CULTOGRAPHIES

CULTOGRAPHIES is a list of individual studies devoted to the analysis of cult film. The series provides a comprehensive introduction to those films which have attained the coveted status of a cult classic, focusing on their particular appeal, the ways in which they have been conceived, constructed and received, and their place in the broader popular cultural landscape.

OTHER TITLES IN THE CULTOGRAPHIES SERIES:

THE SHINING

K. J. Donnelly

WALLFLOWER PRESS
LONDON & NEW YORK

A Wallflower Book
Published by
Columbia University Press
Publishers Since 1893
New York • Chichester, West Sussex
cup.columbia.edu

Wallflower Press® is a registered trademark of Columbia University
Press

Cataloging-in-Publication Data is available from the Library of Congress

ISBN 978-0-231-18723-7 (pbk.)
ISBN 978-0-231-85125-1 (e-book)

Series and cover design by Elsa Mathern

CONTENTS

Dedicated to the memory of Joan Evaline Donnelly

ACKNOWLEDGEMENTS

Thanks to Mandy Marler, Yeqi Zhu, Ian Hunter, Rod Munday, Kate McQuiston, students in my MA class at the University of Southampton, and anyone else with whom I have had a good conversation about *The Shining*.

Also, thanks to Yoram Allon, Commissioning Editor at Wallflower Press, all the editorial team at Wallflower Press, and Jamie Sexton and Ernest Mathijs.

INTRODUCTION: *THE* NON-LINEAR *SHINING*

The Shining (1980) has always engaged me on a fundamental personal level. As a child I had a repeated haunting dream about my father chasing me down corridors wielding an axe. This happened before the production of the film or even the Stephen King source novel (1977). Unsurprisingly then, my first encounter with *The Shining* was a remarkably powerful experience. I remain convinced that there is something absolutely primal about *The Shining*, gaining direct access to childish anxieties in a way few other films have managed. This is not to suggest that the process of writing this book was simply a personal project about exorcising my own ghosts, although that was undoubtedly a part of it. It should be noted that my father indeed had an axe, and used it regularly to chop up wood such as old doors to feed to our open fire so that his family could benefit from the fumes of lead-based paint as well as the warmth.

I was also an only child with a fanciful imagination. But we did have a long corridor in our house and I can remember constantly wondering if there was something at the end of it. I had a period of night terrors that must surely have not been helped by my bed facing towards a door that looked directly down this corridor. Since then, I have been told that this is extremely bad *feng shui*, in that it tempts fate: upon dying you will be taken directly through the door and down the corridor following the direction your feet are facing when lying on the bed. In more recent times I have developed an interest in human perception. Corridors (in buildings and mazes) of course limit vision and have 'declining' perspective, as well as symbolising a transition to something else but also promise the appearance of something at the end of the corridor, or around corners like the girl ghosts in *The Shining*.

Strangely, for a film that has been so important in my life I cannot remember when I first saw *The Shining*. On its initial release, it was rated 'X' in the UK and I would have been too young to see it, so it is likely that I saw it on television first or at a late-night screening in the mid-1980s. It is perplexing not to remember. Of course, I feel like it has always been with me and me with it, making memory hazy. However, I remember when I read Stephen King's novel, under inspiration from watching the film. I was disappointed. I had to concede that King is a creative thinker who comes up with astounding scenarios and ideas but Kubrick's film was light years from the book.

On one occasion I was reminded of what I had in common with *The Shining*'s director Stanley Kubrick. I moved to Europe from America as a child and have retained my US passport. Once when re-entering the UK I was held for a couple of hours at passport control as I had a new passport without a crucial 'leave to remain' stamp. Having informed them that I was a research student studying film, one of the border guards told me that he had once had a similar problem with one of my compatriots: Stanley Kubrick. Kubrick famously avoided travel if at all possible and of course this might have been exacerbated by an incident at UK immigration control but I think I might have been told a tall story. Remarkably, also while I was a

research student one of my friends told me that he ha̲
out in a pub in London and had met Stanley Kubrick. I wa̲
incredulous. His description of 'Kubrick' (thin, English and gay)
confirmed that this was a barefaced imposter. It turned out
to be con-artist Alan Conway, who spent a good deal of time
being bought food and drink by people who actually believed
he was Kubrick, and was played by John Malkovich in the
film about his exploits called *Colour Me Kubrick: A True...ish
Story* (2005). By this point, Kubrick had become something
of a legendary figure. His reclusiveness added to his sense
of being an ephemeral but transcendent presence; in fact the
auteur director *par excellence* in that he did not have a public
persona, which in effect was replaced by his films and his
'presence' in those films. His films thus 'spoke for themselves'
and did so in the most eloquent of terms.

The Shining always spoke to me more than Kubrick's other
films. Was this just that it remained with me on a level of
primal fears or archetypal ideas, or was it that the film seemed
to promise so much more than was immediately apparent on
its surface? *The Shining* stays with me. My experiences with
writing sometimes feel like they have approached those of the
film's protagonist Jack Torrance (Jack Nicholson). Particularly
with respect to this very book. As I spent a week finishing it
sitting alone staring at a laptop in a remote rented shack in
the Welsh Black Mountains. But the only ghosts were in my
head and my sanity survived – just, perhaps.

THE NON-LINEAR FILM

This book has a significant interest in *The Shining* as a matrix
of ambiguities which has begged painstaking approaches to
interpretation and thus furnished the film with its singular
cult reputation and unique status in cinema more generally.
The Shining is quite possibly the most scrutinised film of all

time. In recent years, it has built up a body of cult devotees who look for hidden meanings and in the process understand Kubrick's film on exquisite levels of detail with fastidious care. Rather than simply looking to narrative development, seeing the film as a story that progresses from start to finish, it is increasingly approached in a 'non-linear' manner. Certain scenes are considered almost outside of the film's context and isolated elements across it can be added together to give a coherence not immediately apparent to a narrative-led reading of the film. *The Shining* can appear more paradigmatic than syntagmatic. In other words, it is at least as open to interpretations that 'look outwards' from the film as it is to interpretations that follow the story itself. Such 'non-linear' manoeuvres can use elements in the film to springboard some distance to what might initially seem unconnected material, which is then woven back in with other isolated fragments from the film. This method has borne much in the way of strange fruit.

Like the film's Overlook Hotel, *The Shining* is not what it seems. For a start, many are surprised to find out that *The Shining* is a British film, made in the UK and registered in the UK for tax purposes. For a film that seems so concerned with America it is strange that only a handful of shots were completed in America by a second unit. The film was an almost wholly studio-bound production at Elstree Studios outside London, with an overwhelmingly British crew and a number of British actors appearing in the film. The film is not what it seems on the surface, underlined by the use of British popular songs of the 1930s, as well as the score's domination by European avant garde religious music. The film started out in America with the book's author Stephen King, then moved to the UK with American-exile Stanley Kubrick, from the film's opening at the 'Going-to-the-Sun Road' in Glacier National Park in Montana, transitioning to studio sets in outer London.

The Shining is perhaps an atypical cult film, \
status that has steadily increased since release. A
time, the film has managed to retain a strong ...
profile as well as holding certain art cinema credentials.
Kubrick made a film that works as a mainstream work upon
first viewing but begins to appear different upon repeated
viewings. Clearly, he had a conception that 'mainstream',
less demanding audiences would be accustomed to single-
viewing while more demanding audiences would pursue
multiple viewings of the film and thus discover its dual
character. Many of these interpretations of the film rely on
small details and intricate connections between them, as
well as the seeming connections with events and discourses
outside it. That some coherence can be found in the
teeming sea of sometimes disconnected detail in the film's
backgrounds is remarkable. These interpretations manifest
the 'non-linear Shining' rather than narrative progression and
diegetic illusion. In recent years, this has become a popular
path to follow when dealing with The Shining.

Some accounts of The Shining do little more than flesh
out 'what happens' in the film as if it were some real event
rather than an artistic construction. The film is extremely
fragmented, evident not only in the mixture of some 'high
value' elements and some seemingly of fleeting importance,
but also in that Kubrick's audio-visual style constantly flirts with
discontinuity. Even the most basic dialogue scene is rendered
with slightly unpredictable editing and carefully indirect and
off-whack camera angles. This leads to an experience that
oscillates between fragmentation and coherent continuity,
which frames the experience of the film's representations and
narrative, thus making it into less of a clear story. Kubrick's
approach is, upon close inspection, decidedly non-linear, which
has inspired analysts to approach the film less as a continuity
and more as a series of disconnected fragments.[1] Upon an

initial viewing, we follow and make sense of *The Shining* as a regular film, but on repeat viewings it becomes apparent just how much mental work we have to do to pull together a work replete with non-linear elements that point to or implicate an elsewhere, or suggest ideas outside of the immediate purview of the film. Issues that can seem significant are not 'worked out' by the film and diverse elements that appear to cohere together ultimately do not add up.

WHAT HAPPENS IN ROOM 237?

This is one of the film's big questions, so let us address it immediately. In the novel, Danny enters room 217 and looks around, eventually finding the woman in the bath. She appears to be a dead body which then rises up and attacks Danny, who is unable to open the door to escape. Kubrick's film is totally different. It refuses to show what happens to Danny (Danny Lloyd) in the room. Instead it shows the subsequent activity with Jack entering room 237 (reasons for the change in room number from the novel are discussed below) to find out what had attacked Danny, who has appeared before his parents, bruised and dishevelled. This sequence is the film's crucial nexus point. It is the moment where the threat to the family appears to become more immediate and the audience gets to see the inside of room 237, which has been established as a 'terrible place' and epicentre of the Overlook's negative forces. *The Shining* has set up an intense audience desire for knowledge of the contents of this room, not only with Danny and Hallorann's (Scatman Crothers) awkward discussion of it earlier on, but also with Danny stopping his tricycle outside and trying the door handle, failing to gain entry.

The sequence in room 237 is carefully structured. It begins with a close up of Hallorann on his bed in Florida 'shining'. Then it shows what appears to be a point of view shot of

Fig. 1: Danny 'shines' events in room 237

the open door to room 237, followed by a shot of Danny 'shining' (and dribbling with the intensity of it). Inside the room, we have a point of view shot of Jack's hand opening the bathroom door. We are then shown a direct-on shot from Jack which reverses to show a naked young woman rising from the bath. As they embrace, the camera pans rapidly to the mirror to show Jack kissing a rotting old woman. This is a confounding sequence. After appearing to be encountering an entity (as two women) in room 237, Jack speaks to Wendy (Shelley Duvall) and denies seeing anything. His denial is delivered in a flat matter-of-fact manner rather than with any signs of being an untruth. Perhaps there *was* nothing in room 237?

Initially, this sequence might seem to mark a development in Jack's mental degeneration, or his relationship with the ghosts in the hotel. However, even a second viewing suggests another point of view. Is this sequence in fact Danny's fantasy? The audience is focalised directly through Danny in this startling 'forbidden room' sequence, as he 'shines' events in room 237. We should be careful if we think that Kubrick is showing us at this point an 'objective reality' within

7

the film world. It is not difficult to imagine that entry to this room materialises an entry into Danny's head, and a journey in particular into his unconscious mind. It thus wields images of his primal fears and fantasies. The imagery displays overly positive and overly negative notions of femininity, defined by age and beauty. It emphasises a fear of human (and female in particular) degeneration and decay, and the bath suggests a naked birth from amniotic fluid. Jack's reaction is aghast at the feminine generally, including childbirth. This sequence, as Danny's fantasy, also shows a clear fear of his father and his motivations (here, wanting something outside the family unit), which become much more pronounced throughout the rest of the film.

The design of room 237 in this sequence is utterly remarkable, almost beyond belief in terms of its colour scheme, with purple furniture, and green and dark blue carpet (it has also been suggested by a number of commentators that the carpet design is an abstract representation of sexual intercourse). The bathroom is painted light green-grey and apple green with orange piping. This is a room design from hell, or at least from a disturbed mind. Similarly, when Jack

Fig. 2: Extraordinary decor in room 237

Fig. 3: Unsettling colour and design

later talks to Grady (Philip Stone) in the toilet at the Gold Room, its colour scheme appears beyond reality, being a hyperbolic and overwhelming two-tone red and white. This seems to suggest that in both cases we are experiencing something that is outside of the 'reality' established by the film, either as Danny's fantasy or as Jack's.

One theory about the room 237 sequence, forwarded by Paul Whittington (2012: 54–5), is that it is Danny's mental reconfiguration of the experience of being abused by his father. As the ambiguous heart of the film, does this point to paternal guilt? Has Jack abused Danny and the child has manufactured a fantasy to deal with the situation? Is paternal guilt society's guilt? The mystifying inclusion of a *Playgirl* magazine that Jack reads in the hotel lobby has an article advertised on its cover about incest.[2] In succession, the sequence shows masculine notions of femininity: seductive and then destructive, or at least threatening. There is also the possibility that Jack in this sequence represents Danny, and is attracted and repulsed by behaviour towards him. Indeed, this whole sequence makes sense as Danny's fantasy to deny the abuse.

Throughout the film, Kubrick was interested in imbricating uncanny aspects through the film's audio-visual style as well as through its representations. His cinematic approach here is an explicit stylistic strategy and betrays an interest in medium specificity. Kubrick completely divides sound and image, losing diegetic sound to make the images autonomous but soundless, as if in a dream or memory. He uses straight-on point of view shots for Jack and reverses of him, while also controlling 'the look', which is with Hallorann, looking at what Danny sees, which comes from Jack, looking at the woman, and then she looks back. This is all disquieting when one analyses the structure, with Danny's point of view as a surrogate for the audience and Jack's as a surrogate for Danny. Room 237 appears to be literally an uncanny space perhaps inside Danny's head, but also figuring a 'return to the womb', there to find the horrors (and attractions) of corporeality. The nudity additionally has a voyeuristic character, with Kubrick exploiting film's nature as a simple and basic spectacle. The audio-visual rendering of events not only semi-hides the illusory nature of this sequence's events, but also illustrates the embodiment of psychological states in film style as much as, if not more so than, in what happens on screen.

We never are shown Danny in room 237, only Jack. Is this sequence a fantasy built around Danny's visit but translating elements into a different form (youth and age, sexual desire, the threat of violence)? Perhaps Danny is represented in an older form, as Jack, while his father is represented as a female, both sexual and monstrous? We assume a temporal continuity at this point but there is nothing to confirm that the scene in room 237 is taking place at this time. The sequence also contains discontinuities, most clearly the 'inserted' shot of the old woman rising from the bath, which appears after she has embraced and then followed Jack. This section is not well integrated at all. Indeed, the film would make more

sense if this section had been excised and arguably w
make more straightforward sense if the whole room 2ɔ.
sequence was removed.

Upon closer inspection, Kubrick's staging and construction
of most of the film's sequences display a concern with artifice
and ulterior motive, or at least a desire to make what seems
initially apparent to seem like it is not quite that simple. *The
Shining* contains some complex sequences that are semi-
detached from the film and could indeed stand alone as much
as the film could stand without them (the closing sequence is
a persuasive case in point). These, arguably, 'step outside' the
narrative to some degree. A narrative-centred view of the film
will try hard (at all costs) to integrate these sequences with
narrative development, entailing a glossing over of or wilfully
ignoring of certain aspects. This is in the face of the clear non-
linear sense contained in the film: not only is the audience is
told that Jack has 'always been' in the hotel but sequences
like that in room 237 evince a clear ambiguity about temporal
placement which mitigates against a simple reading of the
film as a story about the Torrance family's adventures in an
empty, perhaps haunted hotel.

2

STANLEY'S OR STEPHEN'S?: PRODUCTION, PROMOTION, INITIAL RECEPTION

This chapter will briefly address Stephen King's and Stanley Kubrick's *oeuvres* and sketch *The Shining*'s production history. On the face of it, *The Shining* is a film adaptation of King's very successful novel, but it might also be considered primarily as a Kubrick film, one which retains little from King's original. Kubrick was, of course, a noted *auteur* director and the adaptation of a horror 'potboiler' seemed incongruous and the possible sign of a 'sell out' in the wake of the bold critical and financial failure of his previous film, *Barry Lyndon* (1976).

On the other hand, King has been disparaging of Kubrick's film of his book. He sees it as a travesty of his novel that has removed some of its principal concerns. He sees Kubrick's changes as significant, indeed defining. One of his main criticisms is of the 'coldness' of Kubrick's film, whereas King's book 'had a heart' (Greene 2014). This suggests that the film and book should be approached as wholly different beasts rather than one being a closely-related adaptation of the other.

STEPHEN KING

King is a remarkable writer who has become one of the most famous and successful popular authors of all time. His books are primarily situated in the horror genre, but not only. Indeed, he wrote the book *Danse Macabre* (1981) about the horror genre and his ideas about it. Many of King's books and short stories have been adapted for the screen. After his first novel (*Rage*, written under the pseudonym Richard Bachman), King wrote *Carrie* in 1974, *Salem's Lot* in 1975, and then *The Shining* in 1977. Brian De Palma successfully adapted *Carrie* in 1976, while *Salem's Lot* was made into a TV miniseries in 1979, directed by Tobe Hooper, followed by Kubrick's adaptation of *The Shining* a year later.

Before becoming a full-time writer, King taught in a high school and also battled against alcoholism: two aspects that recur in his stories. Similarly, protagonists in his books are often writers. Apart from *The Shining* (Jack Torrance), King's writer-leads include *Salem's Lot* (Ben Mears), *Misery* (Paul Sheldon), *It* (Bill Denbrough), *The Dark Half* (Thad Beaumont), *Secret Window, Secret Garden* (Morton Rainey) and *Bag of Bones* (Mike Noonan). Sometimes King has written screenplays from his original writings, and on one occasion he even directed a film (*Maximum Overdrive* [1986], which is now considered something of a disaster).

As writers go, King might hold a record for the remarkable number of his writings adapted for both the big and small screen. According to Tony Magistrale, King has on occasion sold his book rights to filmmakers for a dollar but then taken 5% of the box office takings (2008: 1). He notes that 'by the 1980s Hollywood discovered that any Stephen King work is a bankable project. Few of the 80-plus films from his literary canon theatrically released or televised in a miniseries format have failed to make money' (2008: 2). Films originating with King novels or stories include *The Dead Zone* (1983), *Children of the Corn* (1984), *Stand by Me* (1986), *Pet Sematary* (1989), *Misery* (1990), *The Shawshank Redemption* (1994), *The Green Mile* (1999), *The Mist* (2007) and *It* (2017). Over fifty of his stories have been made into films. King is a prolific and inventive writer, producing gripping page-turners whose startling scenarios can translate well to film and television. However, his own adaptations have been criticised:

> When King authors the screenplays for his own work, generally speaking, there are problems with pacing and focus. The lackluster televised miniseries of *The Shining*, *Rose Red* and *Desperation* are cases in point. All three filmic texts feature teleplays written by King, and each is sluggish in plot development, lingering too excessively over issues perhaps best suited to novels rather than motion pictures. (Magistrale 2008: 3)

Even my favourite Stephen King television screenplay, *Storm of the Century* (1999), has sections in its two-part structure where it appears to digress and lose some of the potential of its enthralling scenario. Greg Jenkins has looked into *The Shining*'s adaptation to the film in detail in *Stanley Kubrick and the Art of Adaptation: Three Novels, Three Films*, and states, 'Like the rest of King's extensive oeuvre, *The Shining* is perforated with technical and artistic deficiencies' (1997: 70).

For *The Shining*, Stephen King was paid a fee for the rights to make the film from the novel. He was then asked to produce the first script but this was not used and he subsequently had no involvement with the project. While executive producer Jan Harlan has stated that King was happy for Kubrick to make whatever changes he wanted to the story (see Wigley 2015), later on, after the film's release,

King became increasingly disparaging when asked about the film, dismayed by some of the decisions made by Kubrick and writer Diane Johnson that thoroughly revised King's story through addition and subtraction of key elements.

STANLEY KUBRICK

Kubrick was born in 1928 in New York City to a comfortably-off non-religious Jewish family in the Bronx. Instead of attending College Kubrick became a professional photographer, working for *Look* magazine, going on to make short films and the independently-financed features *Fear and Desire* (1953) and *Killer's Kiss* (1955). Kubrick then went to Los Angeles to make the off-Hollywood heist film *The Killing* (1957), after which he was signed up by MGM to direct *Paths of Glory* (1957) and then the multi-Academy Award-winning *Spartacus* (1960). He then moved to England to make the Nabokov adaptation *Lolita* (1962) and dark comedy *Doctor Strangelove, or: How I Learned to Stop Worrying and Love the Bomb* (1964). After this last success, Kubrick went on to develop the groundbreaking and ambitious *2001: A Space Odyssey* (1968), which was a financial success and highly significant cultural event. He followed this with the controversial *A Clockwork Orange* (1971), which stylishly dealt with a future of violence and social malaise. Period costume drama *Barry Lyndon* followed, but it was a financial failure and critics were indifferent at the time, leading Kubrick towards the seemingly more mainstream film adaptation of *The Shining*. He then made a Vietnam War film, *Full Metal Jacket* (1987), and his final film, *Eyes Wide Shut* (1999). He died just as *Eyes Wide Shut* was about to be released. His *oeuvre* stands as a remarkable achievement, pitching him near the summit of achievement of twentieth-century filmmakers.

By the time of *The Shining*'s release, Kubrick was considered a great artist working in the medium of film, known for his insistence upon precision and meticulous approach to film making. Yet, as Bev Vincent notes, the pervasive notion that Kubrick was an infallible perfectionist has led directly to the idea that ambiguities in his films are secret messages (2015: 293). To some degree, I concur. Kubrick's films are not without continuity errors and are certainly not utter perfection. However, there is vast evidence that Kubrick thought long and hard about elements in his films, constantly researching for years beforehand and commuting elements, sometimes very late on in the process. Kubrick may not have been infallible and the sort of obsessive who could not abide an error in one of his films, yet he clearly was a perfectionist and certainly enthusiastic and relentless in the manner that he addressed and questioned almost everything that ended up on screen in one of his films.

THE FILM

If anyone should feel the need for me to narrate the film's story, I will sketch it briefly here. *The Shining* begins by showing the Torrance family's Volkswagen Beetle travelling through a visually dramatic and picturesque mountain landscape, using a breathtaking helicopter shot. At the same time, the titles run on screen but move upwards rather than the more overwhelmingly conventional direction of downwards, indicating clearly that this film will be extraordinary. This sequence feels rather cut off from the rest of the film, and not merely because it is the title sequence; it was also not supervised by Stanley Kubrick but shot by a second unit without his presence. It also is the most notable sequence that uses part of Wendy Carlos's score written for the film, as almost all of it, apart from this opening music, was replaced by Kubrick in favour of existing modern classical recordings.

Fig. 4: Opening title sequence

The Torrance family have some issues. We learn that Jack, the father, has been avoiding alcohol. It had caused him to injure Danny in a fit of rage and he is not able to secure a good job. He interviews successfully for a position as caretaker of the large and remote Overlook Hotel in the mountains of Colorado. During the interview, hotel boss Ullman (Barry Nelson) tells him of an incident a few years earlier where the caretaker murdered his family. Jack's family can stay with him and he can spend the solitude concentrating on a writing project. His wife, Wendy, is hopeful but worried about their five-year old son, Danny. The child has psychic abilities, manifested as an imaginary friend called Tony, who tells and shows Danny things. Tony has warned Danny about the Overlook Hotel, where his family are bound. At the hotel Danny finds he has this ability in common with Hallorann, the hotel cook, who refers to it as 'shining'. Once the three family members are left alone Jack begins to exhibit strange behaviour and Danny apparently (we are not shown) enters the epicentre of the Overlook's ghostly presence: room 237. He reappears injured and his father goes to room 237 to confront whoever is there. He sees a naked young woman and embraces her whereupon she turns into the rotting corpse of an old woman. Danny and Hallorann (who is in Florida) are both in contact via their 'shining' and seemingly witness this incident. Jack visits the grand but empty Gold Room and appears to meet and talk to a barman, Lloyd (Joe Turkel), who serves him alcohol, which he has been avoiding for a whole year. Later, when he revisits the Gold Room, he finds it full of revellers dressed in 1920s style. Here he speaks to a butler, Grady, who tells him to 'correct' his family. Wendy wants to take Danny back down to Sidewinder and away from the hotel but Jack turns on her. She hits him with a baseball bat and then locks him in the kitchen store cupboard. Through the door, Jack talks to Grady who appears to open the bolt and free him. Wendy and Danny are then attacked in their living quarters by Jack who cuts through the doors with an axe, shouting 'Honey, I'm home', and 'Here's Johnny!' Danny manages to escape through the window but Jack is halted by the arrival of Hallorann, who Danny had asked to help through his psychic connection. Jack kills him and then chases Danny into the maze in the snow. Danny retraces his own footprints and escapes from the maze, leaving his father to freeze to death. The final shot of the film appears to show Jack Torrance in a wall-mounted photograph dated 1921.

PRODUCTION DETAILS

According to *Variety*, as soon as King's novel was published in January 1977 it was suggested by Warner Bros. as a possible film for Stanley Kubrick, and pre-production moved fairly rapidly for Kubrick's normally slow pace. The actual production was made less straightforward by Kubrick's insistence on shooting the film's events in chronological order, a studio fire that destroyed part of the set in January of 1979 and legal restrictions on young Danny Lloyd's working hours (see Gray 2016).

With only a small ensemble of actors required for the film, Kubrick needed to make good choices. Although he had been around Hollywood for over two decades, Jack Nicholson was fresh from great acclaim and an Academy Award for his role as a masquerading patient in a mental facility in Milos Forman's *One Flew Over the Cuckoo's Nest* (1975). There is a distinct continuity between Nicholson's portrayal of this role and central protagonist Jack in *The Shining*, particularly in his manic energy and unpredictability. Jack's wife Wendy was played by Shelley Duvall, who had been discovered by director Robert Altman and used in a succession of his films (memorably playing Olive Oyl in Altman's *Popeye* [1980] immediately after the shoot of *The Shining*). The family was completed by Danny Lloyd, a newcomer who was six years old when filming began, and who subsequently gave up acting after just a couple of years. The only other character of prime importance was Hallorann, the Overlook Hotel's cook, who shares a psychic ability and connection with Danny. At the suggestion of his friend Nicholson, the part was played by Scatman Crothers, who had appeared with him in *One Flew Over the Cuckoo's Nest*. Crothers was in possession of a remarkable voice. Earlier in his career, he used it for singing (including singing Scat Cat's song in Disney's *The Aristocats* [1970]) and voice acting (in Hanna-Barbera TV cartoons *The Harlem Globetrotters* [1970] and *Hong Kong Phooey* [1974]). Voice apart, Crothers was best known for playing Louie the garbage man in TV comedy *Chico and the Man* (1974–78), although he had also appeared in small parts in many films.

In terms of crew, they were all British. Kubrick used his regular cinematographer John Alcott, with whom he had worked on *2001: A Space Odyssey*, *A Clockwork Orange* and *Barry Lyndon*, for which Alcott won an Academy Award.

Production designer Roy Walker had previously worked mostly in television, while editor Ray Lovejoy had already worked with Kubrick on *Dr. Strangelove* and *2001*, and art director Les Tomkins went on to work on Kubrick's *Full Metal Jacket*. Initially, music composer Wendy Carlos, who had completed gender realignment surgery since scoring *A Clockwork Orange*, and Rachel Elkind were secured to write *The Shining*'s music. Although they ended up producing a whole score for the film, Kubrick replaced the vast majority of it with pre-existing recordings. Other people involved included American Garrett Brown, who was a developer of the Steadicam, and who has provided a good insight into the production process, and editor Gordon Stainforth, who has been a constant source of information about *The Shining*, particularly about its post-production stages. Another contributor is executive producer Jan Harlan, also Stanley Kubrick's brother-in-law, who still gives regular interviews and makes appearances to talk about Kubrick and his films. All attest that while Kubrick may have been an extremely demanding director to work for, he was a remarkably hard worker who spent his evenings looking over the rushes shot during the day and thinking about possibilities for obtaining what he wanted on celluloid (see Joe Turkel in Abbott 2012).

A couple of studio shots apart, almost all the exterior shots of the hotel were filmed at the Timberline Lodge, near Mount Hood, in Oregon. The hotel had been built in 1937 during Roosevelt's New Deal initiatives. It had a room 217 but no room 237, and Kubrick apparently changed the room number at their request. This hotel has become indelibly associated with *The Shining*, to the point where fans of the film make a point of visiting and in recent years it has started to host a horror film festival. Kubrick had looked into a vast number of possibilities for the hotel exterior, and also for the interior. Ultimately, designs for the hotel interior were inspired very directly by the Ahwahnee Lodge in Yosemite National Park, California. However, the original inspiration had been the Stanley Hotel, at Estes Park, Colorado, the inspiration for King to write the novel when he stayed there with his family. (King went on to use the exterior of the hotel for his television miniseries of *The Shining* in the late 1990s.)

Hating travelling, Kubrick did not leave the UK during the making of *The Shining*. A second unit shot the film's opening and exterior shots of the Timberline Lodge in the USA. For a film that appears so American in its locations and lead characters, it is remarkable that almost all of it was shot in the UK. It was a studio-bound production, shot at the EMI-owned Elstree Studios on the western fringes of London.[3] The sets were large and elaborate, with Kubrick requiring all of them to be in place at the same time, including some open-air sets like the maze and some Overlook exteriors. It was a long shoot, taking far longer than planned (see Stainforth n.d.). Although accounts vary of the time taken, it held up waiting productions including Steven Spielberg's *Raiders of the Lost Ark* (1981). Indeed, the latter ended up adapting the high Colorado Lounge set where Jack writes for the other film's snake pit sequence where Indiana Jones has to face his worst phobia.

Kubrick insisted on absolute control and was meticulous in terms of precision with details (see Herr 2001: 54). Stories about Kubrick's behaviour on set surfaced quickly, most notably about his insistence on a prodigious number of retakes of simple shots (see Baxter 1997: 316–7; LoBrutto 1997: 430–1) and his relentless harrying and deliberate pushing of actress Shelley Duvall. These are most evident in Kubrick's daughter Vivian's short documentary about *The Shining*'s production, which was made for the BBC's *Arena* arts show. Both of these aspects gave an undoubted extra frisson to the film, that it was the product both of an obsessive repetition (perhaps a compulsive repetition) and of the reality of the anxiety or what might even be called victimization of Duvall.

According to camera operator Garrett Brown, 'Stanley would seldom respond with anything but derision until about take 14. He did not appear to be comfortable until we were well beyond take 20. Since the editing was to occur entirely after the filming of the production, he wanted at least two and preferably three perfect takes on each scene' (1980). Brown was the specialist Steadicam operator brought in especially for the production. Kubrick insisted on direct centrality of framing and symmetrical composition as much as possible. The film had been conceived with the Steadicam in mind, requiring continuous sets which were left in situ simultaneously, an expensive and uncommon practice in filmmaking. The Steadicam enables handheld camera and was first used in Hal Ashby's *Bound for Glory* in 1976. It is a device that fastens a camera to the camera operator with a counterbalancing gyro to retain smoothness of movement and stability of framing. However, the most memorable continuous shots in the film, of Danny pedalling his tricycle through the corridors, needed innovation. Instead of running with the Steadicam (such as in the climactic maze sequence) weight of camera and closeness to the ground dictated that Brown improvise through carrying the Steadicam in a special rubber-wheeled wheelchair to be pushed along behind Danny's pedal car (see Konow 2013). Brown was using the Model II Steadicam, often in 'low mode'. Working on *The Shining* allowed him priceless experimentation with the device and it supplied a distinctive visual aspect to the film; indeed, the maze sequence could not have been completed without it (see Ferrara 2000: 31).

Kubrick's insistence on precise composition and symmetry within the frame led to a highly singular visual style for the film, along with the consistent use of wide-angle lenses.

Doubling within the frame also adds uncanny effect, from the Grady girls who look like a Diane Arbus photograph to when Danny goes to Jack in the bedroom, and Jack's upper body appears in the mirror but some trousers hanging on a chair make a doppelgänger of his body. All of these aspects furnish *The Shining* with an uncanny, slightly disturbing ambience. Similarly, the design of the overall set to facilitate continuous travelling shots from the Steadicam lead to a confused spatial structure. Indeed, the hotel does not make spatial sense and it seems likely that Kubrick was either happy enough about this consequence of construction or used it deliberately as another disquieting aspect of the Overlook (see Kearns 2011). The most clear spatial anomaly is the window in Ullman's office, which is a physical impossibility as his office appears to be in the centre of the hotel and with no outside wall.

Nevertheless, the Overlook Hotel provides a strong illusion of being an authentic place. I can remember the first time I saw Vivian Kubrick's documentary and was devastated to see that the maze was a false construction rather than an actual location. Technicians worked hard to maintain the illusion as shooting conditions were not easy. The Colorado Lounge set was extremely hot as it required a massive amount of artificial light from outside the windows. The shooting of the climactic maze sequence at Borehamwood studios in fact took place in the summer, requiring artificial snow. This was made from dendritic dairy salt, which is very finely ground and has star-shaped rather than cubed crystals, and Styrofoam, which is an air-expanded form of polystyrene. The mist in the maze was in fact dense oil smoke, which must have been appallingly uncomfortable for the actors and technicians.

A notable effect was the blood bursting out from doors at the elevator shaft, which required gallons of what British crews commonly refer to as 'Kensington Gore', playfully naming it after a famous but oddly named street by the Royal

Fig. 5: Blood bursts from the elevator doors

Albert Hall in central London. For a film about the supernatural, *The Shining* had remarkably few special effects. Indeed, it used only one process shot. This was where Jack looks over the model of the maze and appears to see Danny and Wendy in the centre of it. A shot from above the maze was clearly matted into the shot of the maze model on the table, although the structures of the small model and full-size mazes actually do not match.

Fig. 6: Jack looks over the maze model

As we have seen, that Kubrick insisted on absolute control of the filmmaking process and was concerned with meticulous detail is testified to by a number of sources (for example, Brown 1980; Herr 2001: 54). However, despite constant attendance to the film Kubrick did not 'have the finished film in his head' as Alfred Hitchcock claimed to have. He made changes right up to the last minute before release, and even after the film was released. Co-screenwriter Diane Johnson was surprised to find that Kubrick had cut a scene with Jack finding a scrapbook detailing the Overlook's history, which she thought was crucial to the film's narrative (see Steensland 2011), and the Stanley Kubrick archive has different versions of scripts where it is possible to trace the development from the skeleton of King's original to the extremely different shooting script, although Kubrick clearly made further changes during shooting. Furthermore, *The Shining* had different edits in Europe and the US and initial versions of the film had an end section that Kubrick quickly excised. It was 144 minutes long on its release, but, almost immediately, Kubrick cut a 2-minute epilogue in the hospital,

Fig. 7: Jack's point of view. The maze is different (larger) and Wendy and Danny are in the centre

where hotel boss Ullman tells Wendy that Jack's body has not been found and gives Danny a yellow ball (Jack's ball), seemingly confirming his involvement with the hotel's ghostly activity. The 'international version' (the European release), which was largely used apart from in the US was only 119 minutes long as Kubrick had trimmed 25 minutes. Whole sequences were removed, including the scene at the doctor's (Anne Jackson), where we learn that Danny was once injured by a drunk Jack; Wendy and Danny watching the 1971 film *Summer of 42* on television; Wendy talking to herself about getting down the mountain; Hallorann travelling to the hotel in the snow storm and meeting a garage attendant (Tony Burton); Danny watching a *Roadrunner* cartoon on television; and Wendy seeing a room full of skeletons at the point where she glimpses other spectres in the hotel. Both Jackson and Burton are credited in the European print, despite their scenes being excised. Many other sequences are slightly pruned and two title cards ('Thursday' and '8 AM') were removed.[4]

A 'HORROR FILM'?

While the film mostly follows the basic narrative of Stephen King's novel, an acknowledged 'horror genre' source, Kubrick and Johnson pared the narrative back, while enhancing and adding to it. King's book generally lacked the ambiguities and implications of the film, Johnson's stated aim being that 'It must be a scary horror film without insulting the intelligence of the audience' (in Harmetz 1978).

The Shining has a uniquely ambiguous position: as a horror film that for many defines the horror genre, yet for others it is not really a horror film at all. Stephen King made loud claims that Kubrick knew nothing at all about the horror genre. Others concur. The film's executive producer Jan Harlan claimed that *The Shining* dissatisfied horror fans (see Wigley

2015). Indeed, many reviews at the time of release pointed to the film not being scary, which is usually an insurmountable problem for a horror film. Brian De Palma stated that Kubrick had no understanding of horror, and suggested that he had in reality simply made (as 'a McJob') *The Shining* for money (see Bingham 2015: 118–19). This seems a wrongheaded assessment from a film director whose own clinical technical excellence gave Kubrick himself a run for his money. There are some outstanding horror film sequences in *The Shining*. Kubrick illustrated in some of these his propensity for dramatic effect over narrative development. The 'Redrum' sequence is a case in point. Despite no development of the theme that the book constantly moves onwards, this sequence is one of the best known in a horror film. Grunting Danny wanders around the room as Wendy sleeps, picks up her lipstick and writes on the door. As he becomes more frantic Wendy wakes up and hugs Danny in a frontal shot for her showing the back of his head. In a point of view shot, the camera zooms from a medium shot of the door to a close up of 'Redrum' written across it. This is followed immediately by a zoom from medium shot to long shot back on Wendy, showing her expression of horror at the precise point where Jack hits the door with an axe. This is a tour de force of staging and editing, and leads into the most widely celebrated section of *The Shining* where Jack attacks the door behind which his wife and child cower.

Yet this is a film with relatively little suspense. It is also a film with a large amount of dialogue, and almost nothing in the way of special effects shots. Indeed, it lacks many of the defining aspects of the horror genre and clearly illustrates Kubrick playing with the conventions of the horror film. Some conventions are broken. Pauline Kael, in her *New Yorker* review, noted that, 'The clumsiest part of the movie involves a promise that is clearly broken' (1980: 130). She is referring to the destruction of one of the standard, and dull, conventions of horror films pertaining to a knight in shining armour coming to save the day. Here, it is Hallorann, who has been receiving Danny's telepathic calls for help (through his telepathic 'shining') and then surmounts great obstacles to get back to the hotel. This is even constructed by Kubrick in parallel editing which cuts away from the events in the Overlook to Hallorann's gargantuan efforts to rescue Danny. The 'broken promise' is that he arrives only to be killed almost instantly by Jack. However, some of the horror genre's conventions remain. When Wendy, near the conclusion of the film, runs through the corridors and stairwells of the Overlook, searching for Jack and hoping to save Danny, she encounters a number of ghostly revellers (two men in one room with animal masks and a man with a bleeding skull who says, 'Great party'). In the longer, American cut of *The Shining*, she also sees a room full of cobwebs and skeletons. While the men in evening dress appear solid rather than insubstantial ghosts, they are something of a shock, as Wendy until this point has not suspected that the Overlook is haunted, and her apprehension of these things appears to 'prove' that there was a malign ghostly presence after all. The appearance of

Fig. 8: Halorann rushes to the rescue and is immediately killed by Jack

the skeletons and cobwebs is a shock to the viewer as well, as *The Shining* has avoided dealing in such hackneyed horror film imagery all the way through until then. It is as if the film has told us the ghosts are real and then confirmed this through the most clichéd imagery. Does this undermine its sense of horror? Is this an attempt to pull the film back solidly into the frame of the horror film and away from its earlier ambiguities? Kubrick arguably was parodying some horror film conventions but not burlesquing them.

One might argue that it is a defining horror film. *The Shining* surely must be a horror film as images from it appear regularly in books about horror films. Indeed, Matt Hills' *The Pleasures of Horror* (2005) has a striking still of Jack adorning its cover. However, some might suggest that *The Shining* redefines the horror film, while it equally might be understood as part of that small sub-genre of 'horror films for people who don't like horror films', along with films such as *The Silence of the Lambs* (1991), which are in effect a hybrid of the horror film with mainstream thrillers. Despite the centrality of horror films to notions of cult cinema, *The Shining* is an anomaly in its accessibility and mainstream popularity; indeed, it is both a horror classic and a cult horror film.

Kubrick's *The Shining* is a rarity in that on the one hand it was a successful mainstream film that spawned popular enduring iconography, but on the other is a more rarefied and esoteric object for cult audiences. Its reputation as a cult film has grown immeasurably in the years since its release, particularly once repeat viewings of the film revealed a level of complexity missed in its initial success as a seemingly mainstream horror film and new forms of communication allowed for hothouse discussions among fans. Its distinctive and esoteric cult status is enhanced by its continuing 'naïve' reception as a classic horror film. The film's ambiguities have inspired over 35 years of interpretation, enabled by *The Shin-*

ing working on a number of levels. On one, it is a success-ful and highly popular generic horror film, seemingly about a haunted house. Yet on another, it is a secret message about a variety of weighty issues, and a highly complex art film that is concerned with the sort of profound ideas that are rarely, if ever, evident in easily-consumed mainstream cinema. The net effect is a very powerful horror film that exploits a sense of depth derived from the irresistible appeal to primal psychology and persistent and provocative allusions to wider culture, providing *The Shining* with an unmatched resonance.

The Shining is arguably the most well-known cult film. It is an esteemed member of the twentieth century's pantheon of outstanding films, while simultaneously arguably being the director's most accessible film. Kubrick stands as an auteur of great stature and perhaps for some of his aficionado audiences *The Shining* sits uneasily next to some of his other, less popular films. Yet it is the film's cult status, fuelled by more conspiratorial writing (both published in print and on the Internet), which has given a longer shelflife to the film and has increased its status as a perennial conundrum. Indeed, the film has an increasingly energetic 'conspiracy' approach. While in some quarters the shrill voice of conspiracy theory has been dismissed, I am persuaded that there is something credible in these approaches to *The Shining*, as I hope to explain. The fact that Kubrick is acknowledged as one of the most meticulous of film directors suggests that he intended to leave suggestions and clues in the film rather than these merely being continuity errors or accidents. Ghosts might be perceived by the sensitive in the same way that a historian or ecologist can understand the importance of accumulated events or small changes in obscure flora, and a lay person cannot. A sensitive reading of *The Shining* can tell us far more than a casual viewing. Indeed, repeated viewings reveal different patterns and structures. In some films this is the case more than others. *The Shining* embodies the difference between mainstream film and art. Watching it once, it will likely appear to be a fairly straightforward horror film. However, repeat viewings start to give increasing complexities and implications that initially were obscure or did not appear to be there. Analyses of *The Shining* have tended not to aim for careful and close stylistic analysis of the film, which is surprising as important ideas are embodied directly in the audio-visual style. Everything is not quite what it initially might seem.

INITIAL RECEPTION

Initial reception of *The Shining* was mixed, with some critics appearing confused about what Kubrick was doing even making a horror film. It was popular with cinemagoers but not a rip-roaring success. Indeed, *Film Comment*'s review of annual film grosses pointed to *The Shining*'s poor box office performance in relation to expectation (see Bingham 2015: 118–19). However, this is not to say that it performed badly. Financially speaking, *The Shining* was certainly a success: from a production budget of $19 million its domestic gross was $44.36 million.[5] Many of the reviews at the time of *The Shining*'s release were not glowing, indeed a good many were negative about the film. *Variety*'s review expressed disappointment, bemoaning the fact that Kubrick had jettisoned almost all of King's vision to focus on the pyrotechnic Jack Nicholson (Anon. 1980a: 14). Writing in *The New Republic*, Stanley Kauffmann wrote that the film failed as a horror film as it simply was not scary, a cardinal sin for a film of that genre (1980: 26–7). Pauline Kael noted, 'When we see a flash of bloody cadavers or observe a torrent of blood pouring from an elevator, we're not frightened, because Kubrick's absorption in film technology distances us. Each shot seems rigorously calculated, meticulous, and he keeps the scenes going for so long that any suspense dissipates' (1980: 130). Damningly, Richard T. Jameson in *Film Comment* wrote, 'Did Stanley Kubrick really say that *The Shining*, his film of the Stephen King novel, would be the scariest horror movie of all time? He shouldn't have' (1980). The complaint appears to be that it did not appear 'arty' enough for Kubrick aficionados while disappointing fans of horror films. This is corroborated by Jan Harlan: 'The film wasn't particularly well received in the beginning because people who expected a real horror film were disappointed because there was no resolution. People who expected a good Stanley Kubrick film (a serious matter!), they were disappointed because it wasn't a terribly serious film' (in Wigley 2015).

However, Janet Maslin in the *New York Times* called *The Shining* 'Stanley Kubrick's spellbinding foray into the realm of the horror film' (2002: 2819). Indeed, she went on to write another article about the film a couple of weeks later, noting its confusion and complexities (1980: 1). Similarly, Richard Schickel was positive in *Time*'s review, pointing to *The Shining*'s degree of complexity in its subtext, an element hardly commented on by other reviewers who merely approached it as a mainstream horror film (1980: 69). In one of the first pieces of academic writing addressing *The Shining*, F. Anthony Macklin stated:

> *The Shining* met the fate of several other Stanley Kubrick films when it came out; most viewers did not like it, so they rejected it. Most importantly, they did not understand it in any way which allowed them to deal with it constructively. Also, the criticism it received did not clarify the film. It remained obscure and confusing to its viewers. [...] It failed with most viewers for two basic reasons. It was not the same as Stephen King's

novel, and it was not terrifying in the conventional way
a horror film is supposed to be. So lacking the model
of the novel or the conventional horror genre, viewers
became disconcerted. (Macklin 1981/82: 93, 94)

Writing a decade later, James Hala pointed out that the
negative reviews of *The Shining* were built upon first
impressions, and once critics had seen the film more than
once they had begun to see the film's complexities; indeed,
that this was a film that thrived on repeat viewings (1991:
216). Some have made too much of the film 'flopping'. It
certainly did not fail at the box office, although it may have
performed less well than hoped or expected. But the key
to *The Shining* is not its initial successes but its continued
relevance and interest.

This ends the discussion of *The Shining* as a mainstream
film. It had in effect conventional promotion and distribution.
It could have been forgotten or relegated to cable channel
filler material, but remained in the public mind initially due
to isolated elements: Jack Nicholson's performance (and
especially the adopted catchphrase, 'Here's Johnny!', and a
couple of iconic scenes that are known to both young and
old, such as the door-axing scene and Danny seeing the
Grady girls while riding his tricycle. However, in parallel to
this the film was developing as a cult movie with a profoundly
different sense of what *The Shining* actually was, and also of
the film's value and significance.

3

'PLAY WITH US FOREVER':
SUBSEQUENT RECEPTION

Jack Nicholson claimed that he improvised the line 'Here's Johnny!' as an imitation of the opening of *The Tonight Show with Johnny Carson*, an NBC television show which ran for over thirty years from 1962. This mimicked announcer Ed McMahon introducing the show's host. The incongruity of this popular culture reference at a moment of great terror in *The Shining* is one of the main aspects that have led to the film retaining a perpetually notable status in culture. On the one hand, *The Shining* is arguably one of the most famous films of the last fifty years, while on the other it has stubbornly remained an enigma which has fuelled its cult status.

As we have seen, upon its initial release, *The Shining* was a notable box office success across the world, yet initial 'serious' reviews were disparaging and saw the film as schlocky horror and something of a misfire for Kubrick. However, rapidly a number of writers (for example, Mayersberg 1980/81; Leibowitz and Jeffress 1981) pointed to unnoticed complexities and resonant aspects of the film that 'remained in the head' and were not resolved by the film's narrative. By 1984, David Cook had made a detailed analysis which illustrated how *The Shining* was far more complex than it might initially have seemed and pointed to the film's hotel having a distinctly metaphorical aspect (1984: 2). The critical revaluations of *The Shining* continued as a notable strain but alongside these a more unruly variety of film criticism focused on possible interpretations of the film. These conspiracy-based and fanatical interpretations of *The Shining* have taken place largely on the Internet, although articles were published earlier in newspapers and specialist magazines (perhaps the first of note was by William Blakemore in 1987) which pointed to elements of the film which have remained perpetually confounding. Further significant factors aided *The Shining*'s extended lifetime and change in critical status, perhaps most notably technology and the new culture it allowed (see Hills and Sexton 2015: 1–4). Rather than simply relying on cinema releases, by the 1980s television channels were proliferating and films were more easily seen. Perhaps more significant was the development of home video, which in its VHS format became widespread in Europe and America by the middle of the decade. By the turn of the millennium this was being replaced by DVD discs and more recently distribution has become increasingly driven by on-demand streaming via the Internet. The importance of these home formats was not simply that films were more accessible but that they might be watched with the sort of scrutiny that was not possible in the cinema. VHS and later home video formats allowed for halting, rewinding and even reversing the film. Subtleties and hidden correspondences could become far more apparent. These technological developments have been absolutely crucial for the culture of interpreting *The Shining* and without them it is fair to say that there would be far less discussion of the film. In tandem with this, although in effect slightly behind it, came the proliferation of theories and interpretations that were posted on the Internet, taking advantage of a forum where gatekeepers such as publishing executives did not hold sway over, or control the quality of, material and debate.

There is now a considerable body of critical writing about Kubrick (what might almost be called 'Kubrick Studies'). As he is a key auteur director, studies deal with all his films and *The Shining* is less dealt with as an individual case than it is approached as a momentary manifestation of Kubrick's constant concerns. Scholarship has spawned a few studies of *The Shining* but not many, while writings from a 'para-academic' milieu are rather more numerous, and exist largely on the Internet.

A relatively early piece of academic writing about *The Shining* was Fredric Jameson's essay 'Historicism in *The Shining*', which appears in his book *Signatures of the Visible* (1993). He provides a reading of the film as embodying a certain form of history based on regressive nostalgia focusing on the 1920s, when the 'American ruling class projected a class-conscious and unapologetic image of itself and enjoyed its privileges without guilt' (1993: 95). In a wide-ranging article full of ideas, most of his reference points are literary rather than cinematic; further, Jameson's essay does not feel like it has been the product of many repeated viewings of the film (he inexplicably appears to attribute music in the film to Brahms [1993: 87]). Another significant piece of scholarly writing about *The Shining* was also from a professor of literature. The 'BFI Classic' by Roger Luckhurst in 2013 was the first book in English specifically about Kubrick's film.[6] It is a compelling book, one which concentrates largely on narrative and themes, moving through the film chronologically. As a rich discussion of the film, Luckhurst digs fruitfully beneath the surface using critical theory, yet is unwilling to deal with the proliferating culture of radical interpretations of and conspiracies about *The Shining* (2013: 11). These are also only touched upon in Daniel Olson's wide-ranging 2015 collection, *The Shining: Studies in the Horror Film*, which mixes interviews and essays (both old reprints and new pieces). The same is largely true of Tony Magistrale, a Stephen King expert who has published a large amount about the author as well as books about King's books adapted to film and about *The Shining*, both as novel and as film. More recently, a few books focusing on *The Shining* have appeared that underline its enhanced and esoteric status: John David Ebert's *The Shining: Scene by Scene* (2015), Paul Whittington's *The Shining Explored* (2015) and Laura Mee's *The Shining* (2017). Ebert's book is a detailed analysis of the film's narrative development. He writes and makes Internet videos about a wide range of subjects broadly encompassed by the notion of philosophy and aesthetics. Whittington's book is subtitled 'A Psychoanalytic Interpretation of Stanley Kubrick's 1980 Film, *The Shining*' and gives a detailed close analysis of the film 'psychoanalysed' to show that it is all really about Jack's abuse of Danny. This is similar to James Naremore's analysis of the film as an atypical Oedipal narrative where Danny struggles against his antagonistic father (2007: 193). Ebert and Whittington's books were both published by Amazon's pay-to-print initiative ('CreateSpace'). All of this publishing has sustained an extremely prominent cult profile for *The Shining*.

Indeed, there is a cult of radical interpretation surrounding *The Shining*. In recent years, these have become so vigorous that they almost constitute an industry in themselves, called 'Crypto-Kubrology' by Shawn Montgomery.[7] He suggests this is a particular code that Kubrick has set up, and which is particularly legible in *The Shining*. Montgomery's analyses are available on YouTube, as are many similar works. What is striking is just how many of the videos on the site are dedicated to analysing *The Shining*. Indeed, I constantly have to remind my students that YouTube does not have 'everything', although it is certainly a cornucopia and contains a wealth of material that is a constant surprise. Good examples are the videos by 'mstrmnd' (Kevin McLeod at www.mstrmnd.com) and by Rob Ager. But it is not only on the Internet, as Isaac Weishaupt's book, *Kubrick's Code* (2014), demonstrates. Weishaupt runs 'Illuminatiwatch' and is named after one of the founders of the Illuminati in Germany in 1776, Adam Weishaupt. Isaac is one of the leading voices to investigate current activities of the manipulate secret society of the Illuminati, a shady secret order, somewhat similar to the Freemasons but better hidden and, according to writers on the subject, they include many prominent people and top politicians who conspire to orchestrate world events. Weishaupt's book on Kubrick finds many instances of possible connections to the Illuminati, particularly in terms of the depictions of their activities in his films.

Recent media developments are thrown into relief by responses to *The Shining*. Indeed, we might be able to trace the migration of criticism and discussion from 'analogue media' of printed books and magazines to the digital. Currently, there are extensive websites collating written material and websites containing videos that are also available on YouTube (such as Jay Weidner's and Rob Ager's). In recent years, the dedicated websites (such as the long-running www.visualmemory.co.uk; blogs by Kevin McLeod at his mstrmnd.com; and www.jayweidner.com) have been joined by YouTube 'video essay' analyses and more recently by a wave of self-published books of varying quality. Written material is becoming outweighed by 'video essays', the most prominent of these is Rodney Ascher's film *Room 237* (2012); unlike the others this was a crowd-funded film that had a wide cinema distribution and some degree of acclaim after screening in the Directors' Fortnight strand of the Cannes film festival in 2012. It brings together a number of theories about *The Shining* in a comprehensive and stylish format. Ascher's film is creative in that it pulls together not only clips and still from *The Shining* but also others from diverse sources in an illustrative capacity. The voice-over consists of a handful of people who espouse certain theories about the film, although we never see them and the images form an illustrative and illuminating role in relation to their verbal discussion. It is an example of how debates around *The Shining* have moved out of the Internet to, if you like, more traditional platforms.[8]

INTERPRETATION AND IMMERSION

Esoteric culture and an interest in mysticism and the Occult have been growing in recent years. An esoteric approach to culture requires that objects are approached as symbols, and are *interpreted* rather than having simple accepted meanings and values. In relation to films, the technique of the majority of these analyses is similar. The analyst focuses on details to uncover significance, which is bolstered by erudition (of history and culture outside of the film). Sometimes connections can be of the most tenuous nature, and interpretations illustrate a high degree of imagination, as well as the utter tenacity of the obsessive analyst. No specialist knowledge appears to be required of filmmaking techniques, film theory, film history, stylistic context or underlying ideas of affect. Instead, these are essentially content analyses, looking to add up single instances of objects appearing as well as developing interpretations based upon them. The dominant strategy is to approach the film as a non-linear object. Some seem to simply pick out odd bits here and there and pull them together into a more or less coherent picture which is then explained.

I. Q. Hunter, in *Cult Film as a Guide to Life* (2016), notes that interpretation

> does sometimes rear up as an integral part of cult activity. This is especially so if the interpretation is backed up with esoteric squirrelled away knowledge and is both radically different from what most people think a film means and also (a paradox here) likely, if you go public with it to entertain and strike a chord with other cultists (whose responses are a kind of informal peer review, saving you from making a complete idiot of yourself). One of the best reasons for taking fandom seriously is that films, like academics, may get so up close and personal with a movie as to see more in it than either ordinary audiences or inattentive critics. (2016: 42)

Chuck Klosterman used the term 'Immersion Criticism', which has since been repeated a number of times to characterise this phenomenon. The term describes the sort of analysis that is possible only with many detailed close viewings of a film, the belief that small details are more important than surface meanings and that 'truth' is accessible to those who look long and hard, and beyond the 'light engagement' of most audience members. Not everyone is convinced:

> It's based on the belief that symbolic, ancillary details inside a film are infinitely more important than the surface dialogue or the superficial narrative. And it's not just a matter of noticing things other people miss, because that can be done by anyone who's perceptive; it's a matter of noticing things that the director included to indicate his true, undisclosed intention. In other

words, it's not an interpretive reading – it's an inflexible, clandestine reality that matters way more than anything else. And it's usually insane. (2013)

Some of these analyses do indeed seem very fanciful, but some become increasingly attractive with repeat airings and viewing, much like the way that *The Shining* itself begins to seem something different upon repeated viewings. Ambiguities seem to demand interpretation. Their very incompleteness fires our imagination. This is particularly the case in mainstream popular culture, where ambiguities tend to be marginalised and possible alternative interpretations regularly blocked through closure and explanation in tight narratives and endings that explain and loose ends. Of course, *The Shining* mixes the two approaches. Its context of consumption, initially at least, was as popular cinema. Yet its ending is one of its key ambiguities. On the one hand, it might 'close off' that Jack has always been in the hotel and is in the ranks of its ghosts. Yet it also poses a number of questions (how was he always the caretaker? why did the film not give us more details about the supernatural processes earlier?). For the purposes of analysis, a 'surface-depth' model works well with films such as *The Shining*. It can be consumed as merely dealing with a surface level of activity but has depths which can be dug into, in a manner like archaeological strata, to find the more important level underneath. These substrata can only be accessed via deep analysis, following a complex process of interpretation and after exhaustive viewings of the film. The discovery of semi-hidden textual detail is the key. This process of digging underneath and finding (often incoherent) fragments is massive, time-consuming and intricate, finding textual detail in deeper substrata. The Stanley Kubrick Archive, which is easily accessible, ought to provide a wealth of detail for the generation of new theories but as of yet this has not materialised. Scholars have shown far more interest. Catriona McAvoy has taken particular advantage of documents in the Kubrick Archive, and poses that *The Shining* is a palimpsest of different ideas that makes it particularly susceptible to multiple readings (2015c: 359). The degree of background research and attention to detail that the Kubrick Archive exposes, surely is one of the strongest forms of proof that he was himself perhaps indifferent to the many details in *The Shining* and the configurations into which they seem sometime inexorably to cohere.

REDEFINING CULT FILM?

In recent years, there has been a proliferation of writing and other serious and scholarly activities about cult films (see, for example, Havis 2008; Church 2011; Hills and Sexton 2015). Perhaps one of the most notable aspects of this is the inability or perhaps unwillingness to provide a simple and direct definition of what constitutes a cult film. However, many of the films considered under the banner of cult have similar characteristics. They are often obscure and low-budget productions, often have controversial content (such as 'exploitation cinema') and are not aimed at the general public but at a smaller, sometimes marginal demographic. They are often old films that were or have become inconspicuous, and were roundly ignored by 'mainstream' film culture, so that they were rarely the subject of written studies or seasons at urban cinematheques. Indeed, almost any film can be a cult film but the key is that there is a small but fervent and extremely dedicated following of fans and devotees that wrests the film out of its original context of consumption and repositions it as an esoteric object of continued value.

According to Barbara Klinger, one of the key characteristics of cult film culture is occasional but repeated viewings of the same film (2010: 3). *The Shining* appears to fit this rubric but also goes further, with much of the writing about the film stemming from endlessly repeated viewings and constant close scrutiny of its minor details. In many ways, it bears a distinct similarity to scholarly approaches to film, but also bears the notable influence of conspiracy culture. This combination is what makes the debates and culture surrounding the film so singular. The notion of a cult film requires that its audience has a degree of specialised and perhaps not easily accessed knowledge relating to the film and its surrounding culture; this goes some way towards guaranteeing the value the film in question beyond the dominant 'throwaways' of consumer culture. This is not to say that cult films cannot be produced as mainstream products but that their consumption does not follow that mainstream pattern. The differentiation from casual consumers has to be defining, and suggests a cultural position not too distant from so-called 'elitist' minority culture. Indeed, Mark Jancovich notes that the self-identity an audience derives from espousing cult films 'emerges from a need to produce and protect a sense of rarity and exclusivity' (2002: 309). The aficionado is catered for by cult film. According to Jancovich, Reboll, Stringer and Willis, despite 'cult film' having a tendency to be 'low culture' its opposition to the 'mainstream' furnishes it with 'a kind of oppositional and underground culture that it shares with European art cinema' (2003: 11). Indeed, David Andrews (2013) has argued that cult film should now be thought of as a component of a broader notion of art cinema, with which it shares a clear sense of valuing cultural objects in a manner that evades mainstream consumerism's constant run of novelty and fashion. However, in the case of *The Shining*, this is difficult as the film has a strong popular and mainstream presence. It is in the radical interpretations of the film that the sense of exclusivity is formed, where those 'in the know' are able to see the film in its true light, whereas mainstream audiences presumably approach *The Shining* merely as if it is a well-known horror film with some bits that everyone knows and some great Jack Nicholson moments.

As a mainstream film with a substantial budget, *The Shining* did not follow a regular path to being considered a cult film. Instead, its cult status has increased since release while it has simultaneously retained and built upon a position of mainstream acceptance. Perhaps uniquely, the film has a highly distinct cult status, with its spearheading of 'conspiracy cult' keeping alive the ancient art of hermeneutics. As noted earlier, *The Shining*'s development as a cult film developed with the widespread advent of (sometimes) pan-and-scanned but accessible VHS in the 1980s, followed by widescreen DVD in the 1990s, which allowed more subtleties to be noticed. Around about the turn of the millennium, Internet forums and dedicated websites proliferated and this culture burgeoned. A central agent in the change in status of *The Shining* is the development of what is often referred to as the Web 2.0. This is dominated by highly developed social media sites such as Facebook and Instagram, alongside blogs, wikis (accretions of focused information), and video sharing sites like YouTube. These have enabled the accumulated discussion of ideas, in some cases on very small things, in a hothouse environment that can encourage a move toward extremity and highly-focused obsessive behaviour. The foundational platform for discussing Stanley Kubrick on the Internet was Usenet newsgroup alt.movies.kubrick (formed in 1994), which was discussed by Kate Egan in a study of the change in status of Vivian Kubrick's *Making the Shining* documentary (2015). While this message board is still in operation, it is very sedate in comparison with the material that is available elsewhere on the Internet. It is still interested in Kubrick and his films rather than in connecting them to esoteric culture and hidden information and what Michael Barkun in *A Culture of Conspiracy* calls 'stigmatised knowledge' (2003).

My principal interest in *The Shining* is that it manifests a pervasive cult of interpretation inspiring unprecedented degrees of obsession among devotees. It did not become a cult film through being a 'midnight movie' (although it has often been a choice for late night screenings), nor through being 'rediscovered' or rehabilitated, but through being fanatically appropriated by conspiracy theorists and hardcore film interpreters. The culture surrounding *The Shining*, it appears to me, is not the 'traditional' cult fandom that Matt Hills was discussing in *Fan Cultures* (2002), but part of the 'forensic fandom' that he has discussed more recently (2013: 113–6). While there are some highly developed fan cultures associated with certain films and directors, in some ways, *The Shining* has produced a 'purer' more obsessive cult of devotion, whereby an object is almost openly worshipped, along with its director accorded the sort of respect given to a unique creator. *The Shining* is not seen as a wonderful object of enjoyment as much as it is seen as the solemn bearer of deeper truth, making it a grave and momentous object, which derives its status from its hidden importance rather than any particular form of enjoyment that it imparts to its audience.

Kubrick's *The Shining* might, then, help in redefining the idea of 'cult film', particularly where cult status can be decided through a mixture of reassigned cultural value and obscurity. *The Shining* was made and released as a mainstream film, and has retained that reputation. Yet, at the same time its cult stock has been rising to the point where it is likely the film that has inspired the most discussion and disagreement of any film. Of course, there are mainstream films that have attained a significant cult status, such as *Casablanca* (1943) and *The Sound of Music* (1965) but writing about cult film has tended to be dominated by obscure and in some ways countercultural films as precisely an opposition to mainstream Hollywood. According to Ernest Mathijs and Jamie Sexton, Stanley Kubrick is one of a handful of film directors who have both a cult and mainstream status, dubbing them 'mainstream mavericks', due to their conflicts with film studios or their obsessive control of their films (2011: 70). His films are multifaceted. They are *Kubrick films*, and have an 'art cinema' status, as well as a mainstream popularity and a fanatical cult value. I would suggest that the relation of cult film to the mainstream is embodied by *The Shining*, perhaps in a singular manner in many ways, and this relationship might also throw into relief the place of the esoteric within contemporary popular culture. The mainstream iconic status of *The Shining* has spurred on so-called Immersion Criticism of the film, and the rich and varied constellation of deeper understandings and interpretations. All of this has been fuelled by a sense of the lack of depth in comprehension given to the film by mainstream audiences, who are unable to see past the surface to the truth and profundity beneath. Yet this approach to *The Shining* as a cult film has had almost no impact in academic writing. While there are a few scholarly analyses of the film there are far more 'para-academic' arcane analyses which apply something approaching Medieval Biblical exegesis to the film's many crystalline details.

4

THINGS THAT PEOPLE WHO SHINE CAN SEE: FILM ANALYSIS

One of the clearest strengths of *The Shining* is its un-knowability as to whether it is a psychological horror film or a supernatural horror:[9] whether it is a family drama about madness or a haunted-house tale. Contained within these 'horrors' are the horrors of capitalism, anxieties of middle-age, the relationship of father and sons, as well as the horrors of childhood, ESP and psychokinesis. Other themes include: a psychological 'cabin fever' story; writer's block (creativity as destructiveness); alcoholism; the return of the repressed (forgotten evils of the past); duality of the sort inspired by Robert Louis Stevenson's *The Strange Case of Dr Jekyll and Mr Hyde* (1886); a negative assessment of the protestant work ethic; and the legend of Faust (where Jack declares, 'I'd sell my goddamn soul for a glass of beer'). Although effective as a surface continuity, *The Shining* is a confounding patchwork of allusions and references.[10]

The ambiguities at the heart of the film allow space for interpretation and speculation. Kubrick, however, appeared to have some distinct intentions: to make a film that induces the audience to think that Jack's experiences of a haunted hotel are in his head – Jack looks like he is going mad – but at the conclusion of the film to reveal that actually he was sane and it was supernatural intervention all along. Kubrick sets up the psychological scenario to shock the audience that it is in fact really a supernatural one. There appear to be two important textual facts here: Jack is let out of the locked pantry by *someone*, and Wendy sees the Overlook's ghosts at the end when she rushes around the hotel. See this interplay from an interview with Michel Ciment:

> Michel Ciment: So you don't regard the apparitions as merely a projection of his mental state?
>
> Stanley Kubrick: For the purposes of telling the story, my view is that the paranormal is genuine. Jack's mental state serves only to prepare him for the murder, and to temporarily mislead the audience … The ballroom photograph at the very end suggests the reincarnation of Jack.
>
> MC: Of course there is a danger that some audiences may misunderstand what you say and think that one can dispense altogether with reason, falling into the clouded mysticism which is currently so popular in America.
>
> SK: People can misinterpret almost anything so that it co-incides with views they already hold. They take from art what they already believe, and I wonder how many people have ever had their views about anything im-portant changed by a work of art? (Ciment 1983)

So why does *The Shining* need any interpretation? Kubrick of course might not be telling the truth here. Or at least he might not be telling the whole truth. Whatever the situation, the film seems to pose many unanswered questions, and point to a variety of things outside of the bounds of the film's narrative. It includes many strange 'traces' (left-overs from the novel such as Jack's Stovington shirt and the hotel's ghostly revellers). It has many apparent continuity errors, but they seem too 'obvious' just to be mistakes. Examples include the Dopey sticker visible on Danny's door when the doctor enters but gone when she comes out, and the disappearing chair during a shot/reverse-shot conversation between Jack and Wendy in the Colorado Lounge. As noted earlier, *The Shining* also has an impossible geography, that once you start to notice it seems to become important, rendering the hotel a labyrinth.

Is Kubrick telling the audience something that only the careful and analytical will understand? In King's book, Jack Torrance drives a red Volkswagen Beetle, whereas in Kubrick's film the Beetle is yellow. This may seem an insignificant detail, but in fact may be a pointed 'secret message' or at least an 'in-joke', as Stephen King famously drove a red Beetle. Kubrick is, then, right from the film's opening shot, telling King that *he* is driving, rather than King. Indeed, late in *The Shining*, when Hallorann is making the difficult journey through the snow back to the Overlook, we see another

Fig. 9: King's crushed Beetle

Beetle. This time it *is* red, and is crushed by a large truck on the road. Are these merely chance elements or do they make up a coherent subtext of esoteric messages? Indeed, at times *The Shining* appears almost overcome with its own subtext. This allusiveness is not evident in King's source novel.

ADAPTATION

Kubrick's *The Shining* is far from a faithful adaptation of the original book. Stephen King was not impressed with the liberties Kubrick took with his novel and ended up making a two-part television miniseries, which aimed to right some of the wrongs as he saw it. Kubrick's adaptation of King's novel is certainly free. While the skeleton of the novel remains, most clearly in its characters, location and basic narrative, much is changed. The most striking imagery from the film is not derived from the novel. For instance, Jack's door axing, Danny's pedal car trundling down endless corridors, the Grady girl ghosts in the hallway, the maze, Jack's highly repetitive book typescript, and the slow-motion torrent of blood bursting from the elevators. Indeed, Kubrick's *The Shining* begins with the Torrances driving to the Overlook, which is not depicted at all in the novel. The film then goes on to jettison all the narrative preamble, where, after habitual drinking, Jack hurt one of his students at Stovington Preparatory Academy, a school in Vermont. This comes through as a trace in the film, where Jack wears a Stovington sweatshirt and we are told that he lost his job at a school. The shorter 'International Cut' of *The Shining* even removes much of the story about Jack hurting Danny when drunk, which largely appears in the excised sequence where Wendy and Danny are visited by a doctor. In King's book, the Overlook's manager Stuart Ullman is a more important character who does not want to employ Jack, not liking and not trusting him. In the film, he is little more than a passing walk-on, who interviews Jack and then shows him around the hotel. Kubrick creatively translates Danny's 'friend' Tony from novel to film. In the former, he is at the edge of Danny's vision and appears like a shadow but becomes clearer as the book progresses, while explicitly showing Danny places and foreshadowing events. In the film, he is rendered creepily as Danny adopting a deep, raucous throat voice and bending his forefinger up and down. In King's book, the threat immediately exterior to the hotel is posed by a topiary, where animals cut from hedges loom threateningly. In the film this has been converted into a maze that is crucial for the film's narrative conclusion. In the book, Jack threatens his family with a croquet mallet which Danny has already seen in visions, which is replaced by the less distinctive but more lethal axe in the film. While the film adds the highly memorable product of Jack's hours of typing ('All work and no play makes Jack a dull boy'), it loses Jack's trouble with the wasps' nest, and his persistent reading of the hotel's history in scrapbooks found in the basement. Indeed, apart from one sequence with Wendy, Kubrick's film totally jettisons the basement and the 'creeping' boiler that finishes the hotel and Jack off at the conclusion of the book.

Some elements are dealt with more thematically in the book and appear in the film only as dislocated traces. Like the mallet, the book gives us premonitions of 'Redrum'. The word appears much earlier in the book as an enigma, whereas in the film it only appears immediately before the onset of Jack's violent attack on his family. In Kubrick's film, the spectres are particularly vague, although they make the point that they want Jack to 'correct' his family. In the novel the ghostly denizens of the hotel want to incorporate the talented Danny. The book supplies substantial details about some of these characters whereas the film shows what appear to be leftovers from a more detailed film script derived from the book. For instance, Wendy sees 'the dogman' only momentarily, engaged with another man in a hotel room, after which she sees the 'partyman', who speaks to her. In the novel, the 'dogman' is called Rogers and is sexually involved with then-owner of the Overlook, Horace Derwent. Wendy does not see them at all in the novel. The conclusion of King's original story is changed completely, with the highly effective chase in the maze replacing Danny making Jack forget that the hotel's boiler will explode without constant attention – which it does. Perhaps the most radical change is that Hallorann's efforts to save Danny are effective in the novel and he is not killed by Jack, merely injured, whereas the film, having set up the expectation that he is the arriving cavalry, has Jack kill him almost as soon as he reaches the Overlook. Some of these were alterations made by Kubrick and Johnson to streamline and strengthen the narrative, others they saw as improvements to King's original, and some were motivated by other determinants (for instance, the 'forbidden room' number was changed from 217 to 237 at the behest of the hotel used for most exterior shots, and the availability of a prototype Steadicam enabled and encouraged the film's characteristic continuous extended travelling shots through the deserted corridors of the hotel and maze).

Kubrick's films tend to be episodic and sometimes with little clear continuity between sections.[11] In fact, one might argue that most of his films tend simply to situate sections beside one another, often with little solid sense of direct continuity.[12] This is evident in *The Shining*, yielding a clear interest in scenes and moments rather than in tight overall narrative development. Kubrick's atomised thinking appears opposed to King's holistic thinking, meaning that the film amounts to a palimpsest of superimposed stories and ideas. Furthermore, Kubrick's interest in the paradigmatic (what goes with what at each point) level rather than the syntagmatic (narrative development) means that there is a propensity towards material that works well in the moment but is less coherent as part of continuous development. This might help account for the film's seeming 'looking outwards' to many things in a seemingly heterogeneous explosion of allusion and ideas.

Kubrick and Diane Johnson took inspiration from three sources apart from King's novel: Freud's classic essay 'The Uncanny' ('Das Unheimliche'), Bruno Bettelheim's *The Uses of Enchantment: The Meaning and Importance of Fairy Tales* (1976) and Stephen Crane's story 'The Blue Hotel' (1899) (see Harmetz 1978). Freud's essay broadly concerns the familiar being made unfamiliar; the uncanny is unsettling through being strangely familiar, rather than simply mysterious and disturbing. It is defined by an uneasy feeling, despite things often seeming on the surface to be normal and familiar. This can arise out of nothing but was, according to Freud, the foundation of the Gothic and horror novels and cinema. Indeed, he suggested that the uncanny was able to be more intensely experienced through art and culture than in real life. Kubrick was clear that he wanted to concentrate on producing the feeling of the uncanny, and was less concerned about how this might result in illogical development or confusion in the story.

Bettelheim's book includes discussion of the 'censorship' of the more gruesome aspects of Grimm's fairy tales that took place upon their republication in the 1960s. Using Freud to show how fairy tales engage with primary fears, he concluded that the horrifying and extreme aspects of the stories are good for children's moral and personal development. In the book, Bettelheim discusses the image of the forbidden room in the Grimm brothers' story 'Fitcher's Bird' ('Fitchers Vogel'), which is clearly related to the story 'Bluebeard' (best known in the written version by Charles Perrault). In King's book, this is referenced explicitly. In chapter 19, when he is thinking of going into room 217, Danny remembers Jack telling him the Bluebeard story about the forbidden room (the version with an ogre rather than an aged wizard (King 1977: 169–70). The bones of the story are about a young woman who marries (or stays with) an older powerful man (rich aristocrat, wizard or ogre). He tells her that he must go away for a few days and she can go anywhere in the house/castle but under no circumstances must she enter one particular room. In his absence and with a growing obsession with entering this 'forbidden room', she finally gives in to curiosity and enters. In 'Fitcher's Bird', she discovers a large basin of blood (and in other versions she sees the severed heads of the man's previous wives). The motif of the forbidden room was not uncommon in folk tales and has a clear psychological implication (hidden secrets, the locked unconscious, Pandora's Box). The forbidden room is also often a repository of past things, or things that might be better off forgotten. While King makes direct reference to this story, Kubrick and Johnson developed it with inspiration from Bettelheim. They make it all the more explicitly related to the folk tale with the room containing a basin of blood rendered as a bath containing a corpse.

Finally, Crane's story tells of a hotel cut off in heavy snow, where paranoid cabin fever mounts among those inside, culminating in the character Swede's seemingly unfounded paranoia about being cheated leading to him being killed, whereupon it turns out that he actually was being cheated all along. What Kubrick took from this, apart from the snowy isolation, was the notion of suggesting to the audience that things are a particular way and that a character is deluded, but then ultimately turning this around by revealing that the character's view was correct. Arguably, *The Shining* does precisely this: it suggests that the hotel is in fact haunted rather than Jack going insane.

An unacknowledged influence on the film may well be Thomas Mann's novel *The Magic Mountain* (*Die Zauberberg*, 1924) which is set in a mountainous location where time appears immaterial. This is a snowbound Berghof sanatorium in Switzerland where the book's protagonist is persuaded to stay for seven years. Some other elements are reminiscent of *The Shining*. The sanatorium includes a 'terrible room', an X-ray lab in the cellar, there are constant references to the Grimms' fairy tales, and a dream episode concludes with the killing of a child (by two witches). In some ways, Kubrick's *The Shining* is less reminiscent of King's literary original than Mann's literary ambiguity and thick atmosphere.

If the influence of the *The Magic Mountain* is not clearly acknowledged, one element of *The Shining* is, rather than being an allusion, in fact a direct copy from another film. *The Shining* openly lifts the whole door-axing section directly from Victor Sjöström's *Körkarlen* (*The Phantom Carriage*, 1921). Sjöström's film pre-dates the founding of the horror genre in cinema but as a dark morality tale helped to establish supernatural aspects in mainstream films. *The Phantom Carriage*'s ghostly superimpositions were both dread-inspiring and influential. In one memorable sequence, main protagonist David smashes through a door with an axe to reach his wife and child who cower beyond it. Kubrick clearly based his door-axing sequence in *The Shining* directly on Sjöström's original from this classic Swedish silent film, known to aficionados but probably not known at all to horror film buffs in 1980. Similarly, although perhaps less obviously, Kubrick's corridor sequences owe something to the smooth gliding forward camera movements so characteristic of the opening of Alain Resnais' *Last Year at Marienbad* (*L'Anee derniere a Marienbad*, 1961). Resnais' film is also set in a large hotel with a strange atmosphere where it seems that hotel residents might have been there before. *The Shining*'s references and connotations sometimes are indeed quite evident.

Kubrick's concerns are not only about characters and story on screen but are manifested in structure and visual rendering. One of the highly effective uncanny aspects of Kubrick's film is his concern with framings and space. *The Shining* has a remarkable and consistent emphasis on visual symmetry, containing compositions that regularly appear like mirror image structures on screen. This is most evident in shots of the Colorado Lounge, where Jack does his writing, and the corridors down which Danny drives, on one occasion seeing the mirror image of the two Grady girls in the centre of the frame. Indeed, *The Shining* has a persistent interest in mirrors more generally. Danny looks into a mirror in the bathroom when he talks to Tony; Jack is shown reversed in the mirror when Wendy brings him breakfast in bed; he then looks into the mirror in the Gold Room immediately before the appearance of Lloyd the barman; and then in the pivotal scene between Jack and Grady in the Gold Room toilet. Here, Kubrick creates a spatial confusion, matching the mirroring of the two characters with camera work that confounds. Kubrick crosses the '180 degree line' of classical space, having the unsettling effect of moving the characters between each other's position on each cut.

The film is also plagued by doubles. The ghostly girls, the Grady sisters, are dressed identically in Danny's visions. Interestingly, we are informed in Jack's interview with Ullman that they are of different ages and not twins. However, they clearly are twins (and were played by twin sisters Lisa and Louise Burns). There appears to be two Gradys as well: Charles the previous caretaker and Delbert the butler who spills egg nog on Jack in the Gold Room. In Hallorann's bedroom in Miami, there are two paintings of a naked black woman on opposite walls in a mirror-like configuration. These are made evident immediately before Hallorann begins his

Fig. 10: The symmetrical twin girls

'shining' episode shared with Danny, seemingly of Jack in room 237. Further doubling includes the maze outside and the model maze inside the Overlook, which are unified in a startling sequence where Jack looks over the model and sees Danny and Wendy in the real maze (that nevertheless has a different structure). Earlier, when Ullman is showing Jack and Wendy around the hotel, the character called Bill Watson looks almost exactly like Jack from behind, leading to momentary confusion for the viewer. Parallel to this, there is the doubling of King and Kubrick, which hangs around in the background. They share the same initials and are both 'authors' of the film, although antagonistic and to some degree in conflict about their ownership of *The Shining*. The sheer density of signifiers and discourses that are contained in the film have encouraged a variety of interpretations, some full and 'conspiratorial', others half-formed, and I will run through some of these.

ISSUES AND INTERPRETATIONS

Over the years many interpretations of *The Shining* have emerged and matured. Some of them are inspired closely by the film itself, while others have perhaps emanated more from the ingenuity of individuals and groups. Some of the key, 'canonical' perhaps, interpretations were showcased in detail in Rodney Ascher's *Room 237*, which has given further prominence to them. Here I will discuss a range of the theories and approaches to *The Shining* that either are fairly apparent or have gained traction on the path to the film's cult status as an object of fevered interpretation.

A) Haunted House

On the face of it, Stephen King's book is a haunted house story. Of course, it has plenty of other aspects to it that enrich it and make it something more than that. The nature of King's haunting is not simply that the spirit of a dead person has remained but that the location is the key. King's idea is that bad people and events associated with them can make a place indelibly bad. In a similar manner to another King book, *Salem's Lot*, a house ends up absorbing and retaining evil. King's novel develops this historical legacy and the characters involved at some length, while Kubrick jettisoned almost all references to the hotel's rich past apart from occasional hints. However, Kubrick retains enough references to King's original detailed story to at least suggest he understood the book's haunted house lineage, for example the scene where Wendy sees Horace Derwent in the room with another man (dressed up as an animal). In the film, as this is the first reference to these characters, the audience might regard them as generic ghosts in period attire. In King's book, these characters are delineated at some length and have some significance. Similarly, in King's book Jack finding the scrapbook that details the hotel's past is crucial (inspiring him to write about the hotel). In Kubrick's film, the scrapbook makes two brief and unheralded appearances but has no apparent direct impact on the narrative. Firstly, it is next to Jack's typewriter in the Colorado Lounge, and Jack tells Grady the butler that he recognises him from an old newspaper cutting. Thus Kubrick renders King's detailed backstory for the hotel into a ghostly trace in the film.

The question remains as to whether *The Shining* is actually a horror film at all. In some ways it may not be, but on its surface the film works convincingly as a mainstream horror film about ghosts and a haunted hotel. Films can tell us a lot about ghosts. On the one hand, films are a repository of popular ideas about ghosts; on the other, though, the ghosts tell us about the confusion of perception and cognitive dissonance. They also give us feelings of extremity, the uncanny and the proximity of death and the unliving. This includes feelings of irrationality, fear and abjection. Indeed, ghosts are perceptual anomalies. They defy expectation and might be understood as 'non-contextual': they should not be there. Sigmund Freud showed an interest in ghosts as a metaphor or psychological phenomenon and suggested that haunting implies anything that cannot be directly understood or classified (1984: 150–1). A 'thematic ghost' might be the return of a repressed intellectual, social or political idea, but more directly ghosts embody feelings and perceptual-cognitive responses – both in film and the 'real world'.

Whereas in King's book we are given detailed explanation of the ghosts, in Kubrick's film the ghosts are less distinct. They appear less as remnants of evil deeds in the past, despite Hallorann telling Danny that events can leave a trace like the smell of burned toast, and more like elemental beings, who have 'always been there'. Indeed, the ghosts may be less autonomous entities than projections from the film's protagonists. At the start of the film, Danny has already conjured a psychic friend called Tony, who is the embodiment of his 'shining'. The psychic child has created a double to protect himself, but might he not equally have also created the beings in the hotel? The film suggests more clearly that Jack has conjured these beings from past, as manifestations of his own anxieties about writing, providing for his family, as well as his semi-conscious dissatisfaction with his family. The ghosts embody an anticipation of death, as well as the contradictory possibility of eternal existence.

B) Family Psychology

The other, most immediate interpretation of *The Shining* is that it is at heart a family melodrama. In this interpretation, ghostly elements such as fantasies emanate from tensions between family members. The film is about the collapse of a nuclear family, through Jack going mad, and succumbing to 'cabin fever' through being left on his own grappling with writing added to simmering tensions and dissatisfactions within the family unit. King's book includes all these elements but they are secondary to the supernatural elements, whereas Kubrick puts them on a nearer to equal footing. Some reviewers and commentators have noted that the film is a family tragedy, characterising the film as being as much a family drama as a supernatural one (see, for example, Hatch 1980; Westerbeck 1980: 439). Furthermore, Barry Curtis notes that 'Haunted house films … are closely related to melodramas. They are often about tragic families and the influence of the past on the present' (2008: 16). In *The Shining*, the family may be torn apart by interloping ghosts from the hotel's past, but they are equally torn asunder by issues in the family's past (most clearly Jack's drinking and violence).

There appears to be little holding the Torrance family together. King was upset that Kubrick had put them on such shaky ground right from the start whereas his story is

Fig. 11: The not-so-happy Torrance family

about the degeneration of a good family unit. Consequently, in King's 'writing the wrongs' TV miniseries, he is at pains to humanise the family members, with an errant but good-natured Jack (Steven Weber), while Kubrick's soundtrack of atonal 'cold' music is replaced with a very 'human' choir. As a family melodrama, perhaps the most satisfying interpretation of *The Shining* is that its events are Danny's fantasy and his 'shining' is his imaginative projection of his parents' disturbed and disintegrating relationship.

Kubrick sets this interpretation up for us very solidly: Ullman tells Jack about the 'cabin fever' that can take hold of people stuck in a space they cannot escape. Furthermore, when Jack encounters ghosts (such as Lloyd at the Gold Room's bar and Grady in the toilets) he is looking into mirrors, which suggests that he is imagining the encounter. He is, in effect, talking to himself. The centre of the drama is the family's breakdown and Jack's intention of murdering his wife and son. The book is far more explicit about Jack being possessed by the hotel's ghosts, which turn him into someone else. In the film, Jack appears to be insane and only at one point, after he has murdered Hallorann, does his face take on a visage that appears perhaps not to be Jack. Kubrick removes the focus in King's novel on characters from the hotel's past and re-focuses the story solidly on the Torrance family. After all, the addition of more characters to the minimalist ensemble in the hotel would have added dramatic possibility but removed the focus from the family and the tensions between its members. This 'psychological' approach is arguably a more sophisticated view of the story than a simple one of ghosts attacking the family, and fits in with the development of 'psychological horror' films as a more sophisticated development from the traditions of 'monster horror' films (a move from *Dracula* and *Frankenstein* [both 1931] to Norman Bates in *Psycho* and Mark Lewis in *Peeping Tom* [both 1960]). Indeed, there is a tradition of the 'family threat' story in literature and film. However, here the threat appears external (ghosts) but might equally be internal to the family. The depiction of this nuclear family might owe something to R. D. Laing's negativity about the family unit and its socialisation of children (1967: 58), with its violent unfulfilled father, oppressed mother and uncomprehending child who tries to understand his parents' discourse. However, Danny is certainly the centre of this universe, even if Jack appears to be the film's focus.

C) Apollo 11 and the Faked Moon Landing

An intriguing interpretation of *The Shining* is that it is a coded message about Kubrick's involvement with the falsification of the Apollo 11 Moon landings in 1969. This was (apparently) the first moon landing, where Neil Armstrong made 'one small step for man, one giant leap for mankind', as he put it. This theory about *The Shining* has been propounded in detail by Jay Weidner, in his writings, films and website. It is not an uncommon belief that NASA faked these moon landings; indeed, it is one of the most prominent of so-called 'conspiracy theories'. Shortly before the landings, Kubrick's production of *2001: A Space Odyssey* was, according to the theory, in fact a 'workshop' for the audiovisual version of the moon landings that were broadcast on television sets and distributed as still photographs.

This is all despite a minimal amount of evidence and a direct refutation from Kubrick's daughter, Vivian (see Stolworthy 2016). According to Weidner, who has developed this theory the furthest (2015), and who is also featured in *Room 237*, *The Shining* has a very distinctive secret message

Figs. 12 & 13: The Apollo 11 rocket on launchpad, and then launched

for those that will listen. Weidner points to a crucial moment 58 minutes into the film. This begins when Danny is shown wearing a woollen jumper that depicts an Apollo space rocket. He sits on his knees frontally in the centre of the frame, surrounding himself with his toy trucks. It is striking that the very distinctive carpet design is reminiscent of a launch pad and Danny has arranged the vehicles surrounding and in attendance to the 'launchpad'. In the very next shot of Danny, he appears to be in the same position, but the carpet has changed direction 180 degrees, meaning that the entrance to the pad has now been closed off. Danny then stands up, giving the extraordinary illusion that the rocket on his chest is taking off. Once one becomes aware of the elements added together, this sequence is certainly remarkable. It does indeed appear to be a startling depiction of an Apollo rocket blasting off. Danny and the rocket's immediate destination is room 237, which has an open door with the key fob dangling from the lock.

From this crucial scene, Weidner also points to other isolated relevant points, such as the way that in frontal long shot the stairs in the Colorado Lounge also appear similar to a rocket on launchpad. He believes that the reason for the room number being changed to 237 was due to the distance from the Earth to the Moon being 237,000 miles. Weidner then points to room 237, which he calls the 'Moon room', which appears to be the charged epicentre of events in *The Shining*. He observes that the key fob displays 'ROOM No 237', and suggests that it is a partial anagram, containing the word 'Moon'.

It is not that Weidner necessarily thinks that the moon landings did not happen; rather, he is convinced that the mediation was fake (especially the still photographs and television images). When Jack begins his speech 'don't you realise my responsibility?' to Wendy, it comes as something of a surprise, rather out of the blue. According to Weidner this speech is crucial, as it explains the 'secret message' of *The Shining*: that Stanley Kubrick made the Apollo footage on a soundstage, hid this from his wife, and then included this message to her in the film. Jack must 'honour his contract' in exactly the same way as Kubrick had to.

As we have seen, Kubrick's stated reason for renumbering of the hotel room of King's story from 217 to 237 was that it was at the Timberline Lodge's request (see Ciment 1986). Weidner asserts that this was impossible as the hotel lacks a room 217, and that Kubrick had other motivations for changing the numerals. However, a visit to the hotel's website demonstrates that they indeed have a room 217, which you can book – but not a room 237.

Danny's knitted Apollo 11 sweater is a really striking piece of clothing and Kubrick certainly does not seem to want to obscure it from the audience's view. It is well-lit and dead centre of the frame. However, according to Kubrick's aide Leon Vitali, the director had no say in the style of the jumper and it was randomly brought on to the set for Danny to wear (see Segal 2013). The suggestion that this is a random cohesion of disparate elements certainly seems hard to swallow, particularly after this sequence has been viewed a number of times. Weidner also points to the number of two parallel vertical lines that appear in the film, forming an '11'. There certainly are a good number. Intriguingly, he also notes that the Torrances' precursors in the hotel, the Gradys symbolised by the ghost girls, are redolent of the Apollo programme's precursor, Gemini, with its emblem of a pair of twins. This may be a coincidence but it certainly seems remarkable. Other analysts have taken details in the film further. Jeff Webber's Internet film *The Kubrick Code*, for example, posits that the two eagles in Ullman's office represent Apollo 11 cosmonauts Buzz Aldrin and Neil Armstrong and the three lights in the window of the shot of the butchered Grady girls represents Virgil Grissom, Roger Chaffee and Edward White, who died in the fire on Apollo 1 in January of 1967.

The rumour that the Apollo 11 landings had been faked emerged quickly, and even led to the development of the Hollywood film *Capricorn One* (1977). Although carefully established not to be Apollo 11 but a later expedition, it is clear that the stories surrounding Apollo 11 fed directly into its depiction of the staged landings on a Hollywood film set. Not long after Kubrick's death, a French faux documentary was made called *Operation Lune* (2002). This contended, in a semi-comic manner, that Kubrick had been instrumental in the faking of the moon landings. It is possible that this stoked the fire of theories surrounding *The Shining* and the moon landings, although the film is quite obscure.

D) Native American Genocide

It is difficult not to notice the distinctive designs of the Overlook Hotel's interior. The Colorado Lounge, where Jack writes, is a particularly good example of Native American design being used as decoration. While it may seem slightly strange that modern American culture would celebrate a culture that its thriving has vanquished, its use in this manner is not wholly unusual and indeed has become more fashionable in recent years. On his tour of the Overlook, Ullman tells Jack and Wendy: 'Construction started in 1907. It was finished in 1909. The site is supposed to be located on an Indian burial ground, and I believe they actually had to repel a few Indian attacks as they were building it.' Ullman then goes on to tell Jack and Wendy that he thinks the designs evident in the Colorado Lounge are authentic and based on Navajo and Apache motifs. According to Joseph Bruchac, they all seem to be Navajo, and include some elongated 'holy people'

Fig. 14: The Colorado Lounge

in the style of Native American sand paintings on the wall
(2015: 259). This is the wall against which Jack idly throws his
ball and catches the rebound. Does Jack's activity display a
casual indifference to it (it is merely a wall to him), or does it
indicate active disrespect and ultimately symbolise violence?

Native Americans are conspicuous by their absence in a
film that shows so much of their culture. Indeed, they cast a
shadow across *The Shining*. ABC reporter William Blakemore
noticed this and wrote an influential article for the *Washington
Post* in 1987 called 'Kubrick's "Shining" Secret: Film's Hidden
Horror is the Murder of the Indian'. In this article he suggests
that Kubrick has set up a secret message immediately below
the surface of *The Shining*, making it into a film that constantly
alludes to the genocide of the Native American at the hands of
white settlers, a foundational event for the construction of the
United States of America. Blakemore points out that the film's
concluding image, of the still photograph of the 1921 4th July
celebrations has a further significance. History is 'Overlooked'.
The foundation of the United States, embodied by the notion
of the 4th July, was founded on the killing of Native Americans
and the appropriation of their land by white settlers.

Fig. 15: Calumet cans behind Halorann

Blakemore states that the initial publicity for the film in the UK declared 'See the Wave of Terror which Swept across America' despite the fact that the film had not yet been released there. *The Shining* was released in the USA shortly before the UK, officially being released on 23 May in the USA and 2 October 1980 in the UK. Were the posters merely anticipating the massive success of the film in America? The wording seems slightly curious. Indeed, 'the wave of terror that swept across America' sounds more like a disastrous event than a film release.

Furthermore, Blakemore points to the two scenes which take place in the store room. In both, the Calumet logos (of the head of a Native American man) on the baking powder tin cans are visible, and Kubrick clearly deliberately positioned these in order that some heads would be visible rather than all obscured. In one shot, the logo is clearly visible behind Halloran's head as he stands talking, facing the same way as him and suggesting a direct connection. Later, Jack is surrounded by heads but not visibly rhyming with his, so seemingly acting in opposition rather than in concert with him. The brand Calumet (which means 'peace pipe') was not available in the UK, where *The Shining* was shot, so clearly a considerable effort was made to get hold of the cans. This would seem unnecessary if this was not something of significance for the film. And while Ullman's comment about the hotel seems to be relatively insignificant, as it is not developed, Blakemore notes that it is important in that the Indian burial ground has to be the origin of the welter of blood the bursts out through the elevator doors. This is, he claims, the blood of the Native Americans who were destroyed, not simply in the building of the Overlook Hotel but those who died in the building of modern American nation by aggressive incomers. Furthermore, while this genocide is being 'overlooked', in this metaphorical but charged and repeated image, the elevator doors remain closed in a vain attempt to repress this historical reality and hold back the river of blood.

There are a few other details that feed into this interpretation, such as two pictures on the hotel wall (one of a native American man and another a First Nation design of birds), and Blakemore's ideas have been discussed further in books such as Julien Rice's *Kubrick's Hope* (2008) and Mark Browning's *Stephen King on the Big Screen* (2009). Fredric Jameson noted that in *The Shining* Jack is possessed by 'History, by the American past' (1993: 90). He goes further, noting that the film displays a relationship with the past that is nostalgic for old-time class and social certainties (and 'knowing one's place'), and *The Shining* is not only about the failure of historical representation but also about capitalism being 'out of control'. As the unacknowledged failure of the American Dream, the Overlook, its processes and players, are unable to distinguish work from play, or even life from death (1993: 97). While this approach looks to broad historical processes, rather than specific ones about the destruction of the Native Americans, others have focused more directly and specifically on this. Bruchac's analysis, from a specific point of view of Native American traditions, points to how even elements such as the emblematic discussion of the Donner party and their cannibalism, is usually not thought to have involved Native Americans, although two guides were Native American and were eaten (2015: 252–3). Similarly, Bernice Murphy suggests *The Shining* might be approached as a wendigo narrative, about the Native American elemental spirit that possesses people, converting them into cannibals who then see all other fellow humans as potential prey (2015: 219–20).

The Shining is without doubt about the past fighting for a place in the present, and indeed appears to be about the past's ability to attack the present. Design and recorded culture, like organic memory, can be an externalisation of what we think we remember. This retains a shadowy life for lost objects, which can return as manifestations of what Freud referred to as the 'return of the repressed' (1964: 80).

E) The Holocaust's Shadow

According to Geoffrey Cocks, in *The Wolf at the Door: Stanley Kubrick, History and the Holocaust* (2004), Kubrick had wanted to make a film about the Holocaust for a long time. This unrealised project was to be called 'Aryan Papers'. As a cultural historian, Cocks has charted the cultural impact of the Holocaust, and suggests that a notable influence of aspects of the Holocaust is evident in all of Kubrick's films. As a New York Jew it was inevitable that the Holocaust would have occupied Kubrick's mind to some degree from time to time but Cocks is at pains to find its influence and defining character at all points in Kubrick's work, and he finds repeated references in *The Shining* to '42', a thesis presented in detail not only in two books (one edited) but also in Rodney Ascher's *Room 237.*

What is the significance of '42'? The Wannsee Conference in January of 1942, led by Reinhard Heydrich and Adolf Eichmann, is accepted to be the official point where the Nazi regime decided on 'the Final Solution to the Jewish Question', and moved towards mechanised extermination through concentration camps. This programme went full speed ahead in that summer. Hence, Cocks notes the importance of *Summer of '42* (1971) being on television in the film (2004: 232–3). After all, rather than simply being an indicator of the popular culture banality of entertainment consumed by Wendy, this film seems to have no real relevance for *The Shining*. Indeed, while the film and book (by Herman Raucher) were massively successful in the early 1970s, interest boiled very quickly and by the time of *The Shining*'s release they were a distant, blurred memory, if that. Michel Legrand's soupy romantic music is now far better known than the film in which it appeared.

Cocks points to many instances of the number 42 in the film. Some appear clear, while others are less so. For example, there are 42 cars in the Overlook parking lot in an early aerial shot; it appears on a car number plate, and he even notes that the individual integers of room 237 make 42 when multiplied together. Numerology is a common interest of obsessive polymaths, and while Kubrick may or may not have inserted 42 obsessively across *The Shining*, Cocks seems to find it and versions of it wherever he looks. Similarly, oblique references to Nazi Germany and the Holocaust are discovered throughout the film. For example, Cocks notes Jack's quotation from the children's story of the three little pigs as he cuts down the door of the family quarters. He relates this to the 1933 *Silly Symphonies* film *The Three Little Pigs*, which was not only made at the same time as Hitler's accession to power in Germany but also includes some anti-Semitic representations of the wolf, who is threatening at the door. According to Cocks, there are constant reminders of the Nazis, including the final image, where the slow crossfade makes a momentary superimposition where Jack's hair remains from the smaller scale picture in the larger of final pic seemingly adding a ghostly Hitler-style moustache for a fraction of a second.

The Nazi connection is possibly evident in *The Shining*'s choice of incidental music. Kubrick chose existing modernist classical music (concert hall music), written by composers who had felt some impact from the Nazis. György Ligeti, a Hungarian Jew, was a slave labourer in a camp during World War II, and lost both his father and brother in the Holocaust. An excerpt from his *Lontano* marks the points where 'shining' takes place in the film. Hungarian composer Béla Bartók was a vocal opponent of the Nazis. His piece of music used in the film, the *Music for Strings, Percussion and Celesta*, had its premiere in Basel, Switzerland, at a time when Hitler was German premier and had re-occupied the demilitarised Rheinland a couple of months earlier, and was on his way to annexing surrounding countries over the next couple of years. Krzysztof Penderecki composed a significant proportion of the music used in *The Shining*. As a child in Poland he experienced Nazi occupation and ended up composing some music *in memoriam* of the victims of the Holocaust (most clearly in his *Dies Irae* of 1967 and *Kadisz* of 1974 – although neither of these pieces appear in *The Shining*, which they surely would have if Kubrick had wanted the film to 'be about the Holocaust'). The musical connection indeed might be overplayed, particularly as it does not register that one of the most prominent musicians used in the film, singer Al Bowlly was killed by the Nazis, by a Luftwaffe bomb in 1941 (if only it had been 1942…). It is worth noting that in Douglas Adams' *Hitchhiker's Guide to the Galaxy* (originally broadcast on BBC radio in 1978), the number '42' is the answer to the question of life, the universe and everything.

As a professor of History who specialises in Nazi Germany, Cocks is hardly an irrational figure. He certainly has enumerated pieces of evidence but perhaps they do not necessarily add up to a coherent line of interpretation. Rather, they seem more like fragments that point in a certain direction and Cocks seems well aware of this. Kubrick may have desired to make a 'Holocaust film' but found it impossible to deal with the Holocaust directly. It is a moot point that the magnitude of the Holocaust might make it too great for adequate representation. Consequently, it could remain as a constant trace, a memory of terrible things in the past – much like the hotel's ghosts in *The Shining*. Indeed, history can only exist in the present in human minds as it no longer survives, although it can make a spectral return like the ghosts in Kubrick's film. In King's book, the ghosts have been evil and we are left in no doubt that they have distinct bad intentions. In Kubrick's film, the ghosts are actually rather banal. Mostly, they are images of past people doing unremarkable things. One is reminded of Hannah Arendt's phrase 'the banality of evil' that she used as the subtitle to her 1963 book about Nazi war criminal Adolf Eichmann, who she interviewed during his trial and wait for execution in Jerusalem.

Cocks is a practitioner of so-called 'psychohistory' (and co-edited a volume with that title), which advocates the application of psychological method and theories to history. Although the impact of this approach on mainstream academic history has been minimal, it certainly can yield remarkable new perspectives on history and historicism. In the BFI Classic on *The Shining*, Roger Luckhurst's mis-spelling of Ullman's name as 'Ullmann' makes him appear more Germanic and less possibly Jewish (2013: 9). Perhaps this was a subliminal spelling mistake, registering the unconscious impact and undercurrent of transposed Holocaust memory in *The Shining*.

Is it stretching things too far to suggest there is a subtext in *The Shining* about the Holocaust? Kubrick's Jewish background and long-held desire to make a film about the Holocaust could well have fed into *The Shining*, in the desire to make a film whose horror has oblique associations with this most horrific of events. Cocks goes further, though, suggesting that Kubrick had become utterly bored making *Barry Lyndon* and wanted to make a film like no other before, under the inspiration of writings about subliminal persuasion. Kubrick certainly had his own reminder about the Nazis in that his wife's uncle was Veidt Harlan, who was one of the top film directors in Nazi Germany, and one could make a case that the use of the Volkswagen was as much inspired by the company's full involvement in the Nazi regime in Germany as by King's use of the vehicle. The Holocaust casts a long and large shadow. Hallorann tells Danny, 'When something happens it can leave a trace of itself behind. Say, like if someone burns toast.' Impact on culture may not be instantly apparent, but the magnitude of the Nazi genocide was such that it continues to hang over us and leave traces even in places where it might least be expected. While it is difficult to see *The Shining* as directly 'about' the Holocaust, on the level of persistent but low-level implication, Cocks might well have something in that an atrocity of such magnitude would cast a shadow across much subsequent culture.

OTHER THEORIES AND INTERPRETATIONS

Some of these following explanations perhaps do not quite constitute fully coherent interpretations but they emanate from detailed scrutiny of *The Shining*, which allows notable patterns to become evident. Indeed, the film appears to be full of fragmentary part-discourses and small autonomous patterns that add up to indeterminate conclusions.

For example, judging by *The Shining*, Kubrick clearly had an interest in Canadian artist Alex Colville's paintings, and indeed an interest in Canadian art more generally. A number of distinctive paintings by Canadian artists adorn the walls of the Overlook Hotel. Apart from Colville's work, Fredrick H. Varley's *Stormy Weather, Georgian Bay* from 1920; two by Norval Morrisseau, whose *Flock of Loons* appears twice in different places; Paul Peel's *After the Bath*; A. Y. Jackson's *Red Maple* from 1914; as well as paintings by J. E. H. MacDonald and Tom Thomson all appear (see Wlasenko n.d.). The Overlook also has a number of pictures on the walls of what appear to be European, particularly British, birds. It seems remarkable that Kubrick would have the set decorated with obscure but striking Canadian art. It might be possible that a random 'job lot' of Canadian art was procured for the film but this hardly seems likely given Kubrick's reputation for precision. The degree of interest Kubrick took in details in his films was clear. Morrisseau's *Flock of Loons* is a First Nation (Native American) style design in keeping with the hotel's myriad elements of Native American design. Many of the paintings are landscapes but Alex Colville's paintings

Fig. 16: Wendy passes Colville's 'Cow and the Moon'

appear more important. They have a haunting quality to them, with two in the hotel being *Cow and the Moon* and *Horse and Train*. Wendy passes *Cow and the Moon* on the Overlook stairs near the conclusion when she sees the hotel's ghosts. *Cow and the Moon* has an almost mystical tone to its basic figurative depiction of a prone cow from behind looking at a full moon. If this had appeared in room 237 it would be support for the 'Moon room' theory! Instead, Colville's *Dog, Boy and the St. John River* appears there, partially obscured, half-hidden behind a table lamp, and seen in a mirror. It depicts a quietly disturbing scene: a boy carrying a gun with a dog standing behind him face out across the river. His face is hidden and they appear to be looking at or for something, with the impression being that it might be a threat to them. The picture's place, at the entrance to room 237, mirrors Jack (and Danny before him, which we do not see) looking with some trepidation into the room that inspires dread.

The most immediately disturbing Colville picture that appears in *The Shining* is that of a train steaming down a railway track and a horse running full pelt along the track towards it. *Horse and Train* (from 1954) appears in the apartment hall in the deleted scene in which Wendy and the paediatrician discuss Danny. This is an utterly distressing picture, telling of an inevitable catastrophic impact. Perhaps it is suggesting that the paediatrician's words of comfort are useless and disaster is inevitable. The painting *Woman and Terrier* is on the wall in the Torrances' apartment behind Wendy as she answers the phone to find that Jack has got the job. Like many of Colville's paintings there is something seemingly amiss in his staging. The woman has her face obscured by the seemingly indifferent dog that looks away to the side.

As Juli Kearns (2015) points out, another of Colville's paintings seems to have a striking relationship with *The Shining* and yet does not appear in the film at all. His painting *May*

Day depicts an unhappy, perhaps distraught, woman leaning against a static yellow Volkswagen Beetle in a landscape dominated by fir trees, such as in a mountainous terrain. *The Shining* starts by showing the Torrances' yellow Volkswagen Beetle traversing the dramatic mountainous landscape on the way to the Overlook Hotel. The woman has long, straight black hair and could be Wendy from the film. It is almost as if Kubrick has taken Colville's painting from 1970 as a partial inspiration for his film. The title *May Day* probably relates less to a date than to the distress call (mayday, or *m'aidez*), and it is not difficult to imagine that something terrible has happened to the woman in the picture, who looks pensive and exhausted. Had Kubrick used this picture in *The Shining* it might somehow have seemed *too* obvious, and not consonant with the regime of constant oblique allusion in the film.

A line of analysis forwarded by Rob Ager (2012) is that Kubrick included a submerged discourse in *The Shining* about the Gold Standard and the USA's economic policy in the interwar years. He points to the centrality of the Gold Room in Kubrick's film but its absence in the book. Jack and barman Lloyd talk about credit, and the Kubrick Archive contains the prop scrapbook that hardly appears in the film, which strangely includes clippings about finance and economics. This is a real 'hidden meaning' interpretation, forwarded by Ager in one of his Internet film analysis videos (at collativelearning. com). The Federal Reserve replacement of the gold standard means for Jack that, 'Your money's no good here', as his old money could not be exchanged for gold any more. Ager sees the film's final still image as including the first president of the Federal Reserve and potentially other US politicians and bankers from the interwar years when the money ceased to mean redeemable gold.

Ager's is an interesting and oblique development from the material on the surface of *The Shining*, whereas some interpretations have stuck with more traditional 'occult' aspects of the film. Isaac Weishaupt (2014), in particular, sees the film as being about the shady organisation of world-controllers, the Illuminati. He interprets Kubrick's films as all having some element of criticising this undemocratic, transnational top-secret group who dictate world events. The Overlook, perhaps more in King's version than Kubrick's, appears to be run by shadowy hidden bosses who are involved in occult animistic practices. One of the notable occult moments is the final still photograph on the wall. Here Jack, at the front of the crowd of people, makes the one-arm-up-and-one-arm-down sign that signifies 'as above so below', which has been one of the most notable body symbols of esoteric culture and the occult.

CULTURE WARS

Something less than an 'interpretation' of *The Shining* that I developed in an earlier book (see Donnelly 2005) points to music in the film which, bolstered by the ordering of other elements, structures a persistent concern with cultural value and status. At heart, the film is a surface skin of mass culture hiding an underneath of complex and ambiguous high art. This is also manifested as an ordering principle across the film itself. *The Shining*'s music mixes so-called 'art music' (which has the character of being about art, 'art for art's sake') and popular music (which is about 'mass culture'). Most of the film's incidental music was derived from recordings of modernist classical concert hall music, while the popular music in the film is directly associated with the ghosts and the Overlook itself, and consists of songs from the 1930s.

Cultural status is a clear means of structuration in *The Shining*. Jack is a creative writer, and is writing an avant garde novel which his family cannot even begin to comprehend (upon seeing the manuscript, Wendy is overwhelmed and incredulous). On the other hand, Danny likes TV cartoons, Jack nursery rhymes (the three little pigs), and there are Disney characters in Danny's room (moving Dopey sticker on door, a Goofy doll on the wall dressed in a manner that mirrors and mimics Wendy). Jack's degeneration involves him adopting (and quoting in an arch postmodernist manner) clichéd catchphrases from popular culture. This marks something on the way to a debate about cultural value, and corrosive aspects of culture. While images may be clear indication, the strongest indication of cultural status and value are in the film's musical score.

In a number of his films, Kubrick used existing recordings almost as a signature. The music he chose is sometimes extremely powerful, on occasion to the point where it can overpower the other elements of the film, perhaps a little like a spice in food. Interestingly, though, much of the music used in *The Shining* had already been used elsewhere, indeed in earlier film and television texts, sometimes fairly recently. Documents in the Stanley Kubrick Archive show how much background research Kubrick did into the music. It also illustrates how far he changed his mind, initially looking into using Scott Joplin. This indeed appears strange, as *The Sting* (1973) had monopolised Joplin's piano music just a few years earlier. The main melody of Wendy Carlos's title theme is derived directly from the *Dies Irae*, the medieval mass of the dead (although it is often assigned by critics to Hector Berlioz's *Symphonie Fantastique*, which had also used the *Dies Irae*). By the time of *The Shining* it had become a staple of horror films and arguably known for that connection more than any religious association. Kubrick had already used Ligeti's music prominently in *2001*. *Lontano,* an excerpt of which is used in the film at points where the 'shining' takes place, appeared on an album tied-in with *2001* called *Music Inspired by 2001*. Krzysztof Penderecki's *Polymorphia* had been used in William Friedkin's *The Exorcist* (1973), which has a similar range of pre-existing pieces to *The Shining*. Indeed, the character of the soundtrack for both films bears perhaps more than superficial similarity. The excerpt that appears repeated in *The Shining* and functions almost like a theme for the film is a section of the slow movement from Bartók's *Music for Strings, Percussion and Celesta*. I was interested to find that this very section had been used in an episode of British television science fiction serial *Doctor Who*, in the story 'The Web of Fear' (1968). Kubrick may well have seen this on television and may have also seen an earlier use on American television, as the opening theme to *The Vampira Show* (1954–55), where the eponymous gothic character introduced films. Similarly, it is quite possible that Kubrick had seen an earlier use of Al Bowlly's songs in a dramatic environment. In 1978, the BBC's production of the Dennis Potter television play *Pennies From Heaven* used old songs in a startling manner, with actors lip-synching to them like in an integrated musical, and including one song sung by Al Bowlly.

In fact, the old songs in *The Shining* are far from straightforward and pose a number of questions and have interesting implications. Firstly, the songs are British rather than American. This is curious. American songs from this period were bigger hits and would have been far more likely to be heard in the hotel. This seems like a conscious choice rather than a random element. However, British music at this point had a reputation for a 'sweeter' sound than its American counterpart. This means more restrained and less influenced by 'hot' jazz (see Mawer 2008: 275). This suggests that it is 'whiter' than American popular music, which might underscore the racial division of the film. Britishness might also represent a retrogressive idea of the initial colonisers of the land of America. This is also part of the trace of Britishness, or rather Englishness, across the film that might reflect or give a clue about the film's origins.

In addition to these being British songs, they also appear to be anachronistic. The picture at the end of the film is dated '1921' and the final shots are accompanied by 'Midnight, the Stars and You'. The dating implies that the ghostly activity in the hotel takes place at the start of the second decade of the twentieth century. Yet the songs are all from over a decade later. It is unlikely Kubrick was indifferent to history here. Is this an implication of another unacknowledged era of activity among the hotel's ghostly occupants?

Also, 1921 seems an interesting point for music and popular culture more generally. It is just before the large explosion of mass culture of the 1920s, which established the terrain of popular culture industries that broadly is still in place today. Indeed, this is the point before the 'Roaring Twenties' accelerated mass culture and 'pop' culture, and seemingly pushed art culture to the margins. Two of *The Shining*'s songs are sung by Al Bowlly (with the Ray Noble Orchestra): 'Midnight, the Stars and You' (from 1932) and 'It's All Forgotten Now' (from 1934). Bowlly is now seen as possibly the first 'pop singer' (he was known as 'The Big Swoon') at a time where band leaders were known to audiences but names of their singers were not. Bowlly was also the first crooner, using a more intimate and expressive singing style which was enabled by the increasing use of electric microphones in the early 1930s. This turn from the 1920s to the 1930s emphasises the point not only where mass culture becomes established and dominant, but also of America coming to world domination through mass culture. In a way, this might be construed as the foundation of the 'America' that is known across the world: not the politically and ethnically diverse collection of states constituting the USA, but the cultural entity of 'America'.

One narrative-based theory is that *The Shining* can be

'made into sense' if we become aware of changes in register in the film, that the film oscillates between being diegetic 'reality' and being the story in the book that Jack is writing. According to YouTube's Marten GO there are key signals that we are almost imperceptibly shifting between the novel's fantasy and the film's diegesis, such as Jack's burgundy jacket, a different tricycle, the typewriter changing colour (beige then grey), and the presence then absence of the wooden sculpture on the table in the Colorado Lounge (GO n.d.). Another theory finds both logic and massive significance, and involves the presence of a cabalistic numerology system in the film which points to the date of the Mayan prediction of the Apocalypse (see Jonny53 2008).

To summarise this chapter, *The Shining* manages simultaneously to be a popular mainstream film and a high-art style conundrum, thus embodying precisely a debate between the poles of what some might call 'elitist' high art and mindless mass/popular culture. We should remember, of course, that each is emblematic for an ideological position: elitism/integrity on the one hand and populism/trash on the other. A sense of cultural divide between film aesthetics is also evident, mixing on the one hand the sort of popular imagery and storyline that have made the film a perennial favourite, with, on the other, more esoteric and ambiguous content but also film style derived more from art cinema or avant garde film. The camerawork and staging in *The Shining* is striking and becomes all the more apparent on repeated viewings. Camera movement is often smooth and continuous, using the Steadicam and staging for its capabilities. Consistently, Kubrick aims for symmetrical compositions, with this at times becoming almost overwhelming. This is, of course, a rarity in mainstream cinema, where Kubrick's directly-centred staging in sets built to allow fully-symmetrical mirror-image compositions would be considered far too mannered and alienating. Conventional composition tends to aim consistently at being 'off centre' to seem less 'staged' and more real. Kubrick's approach is what David Bordwell has called parametric narration (1985: 283). This is where conventional concerns for filming action, based on standard shots showing characters, are dictated by the narrative development of character interaction and events. Instead, the filmmaker uses a pre-planned approach to camera movement and staging that is an almost autonomous strategy rather than necessarily being dictated by the action. The effect of adopting such a strategy is that content is de-emphasised and underlying or not immediately apparent structure is brought to the fore. Kubrick bases *The Shining* on slow tracking and shots that move in on characters or follow them, usually from behind (until this is reversed in the concluding sequence). This focus on style underlines the notion that there is something more going on in the film, and that the story and characters are not necessarily the focal point of the film's significance.

However, Leon Vitali, Kubrick's aide during production, dismissed intentionality in many of the aspects that have become pivotal to different interpretations: 'Mr. Vitali said he never spoke with Kubrick about any larger meaning in *The Shining.* "He didn't tell an audience what to think or how to think", he said, "and if everyone came out thinking something differently that was fine with him. That said, I'm certain that he wouldn't have wanted to listen to about 70, or maybe 80 percent" of *Room 237*. ... Because it's pure gibberish' (Segal 2013). Yet Kubrick, much like his films, was not fully transparent. Michael Herr noted, 'Stanley always acted like he knew something you didn't know' (2001: 4). The 'intentional fallacy' points to how authorial intention is immaterial in the face of what a cultural object actually achieves. So is Kubrick's view determining or irrelevant? Kubrick said: 'A story of the supernatural cannot be taken apart and analysed too closely.

The ultimate test of its rationale is whether it is good enough to raise the hairs on the back of your neck. If you submit it to a completely logical and detailed analysis it will eventually appear absurd. ... People can misinterpret almost anything so that it coincides with views they already hold. They take from art what they already believe' (Ciment 1983). Some of the interpretations outlined above appeal to views held widely already. But Kubrick clearly used 'subliminals' in the film, the shapes of faces appearing in doors, for example, and peppered the film with small enigmas and pieces of information with possible significance.

Are all these details mere coincidences? It seems unlikely. Are there any other films that have the degree of confounding detail that appears to suggest something else? While there may be few films that have had the level of meticulous scrutiny that *The Shining* has received, there is a good reason for this: the film contains so much allusion and implication that it is almost inconceivable that these notable elements and fragments are merely in existence by chance, let alone that their coherence together should be something merely in the imagination of the fevered film analyst. That Kubrick was extremely interested in detail is clear. For instance, the television in the Torrances' quarters in the Overlook has no cable at all going to it. This is clearly not a mistake but by design. It is not telegraphed and only noticed with careful viewing. On an unconscious level, though, it could well make us realise that even the most normal moments in the film are far from being so. Furthermore, it is the sign of an authorial presence. Not in a crass and overt manner but in a subtle manner that captures the attention of those who are looking carefully. Similarly, it also suggests that things are not all about the illusion of the 'real' film world on screen, and this encourages a looking beyond the immediacy of the story, characters and events, into what lies beneath and behind.

5

ACADEMIC BULLSHIT: THE PLACE OF THE FILM

Referring to the film *Room 237* and its analyses of *The Shining*, Stephen King declared it 'academic bullshit' (see Greene 2014). My initial response to this would be that these interpretations may be bullshit but they are certainly not academic. Indeed, academic writing has been unwilling to engage with these radical interpretations of so-called Immersion Criticism. King's dismissal of the varied interpretations and conjectures is, of course, equally a dismissal of Kubrick's film and reassertion of his original novel. But all the interest appears to be in Kubrick's film rather than King's book. Indeed, there remains something of an authorship contest or perhaps unofficial 'debate'. Almost all of the film's differences were decried by King, who saw his original ideas and intentions as having been displaced. As noted earlier, in 1997, *The Shining* was remade as a television miniseries by King in an attempt to wrest the original sense of the story back from the film, expending much effort attempting to escape the shadow of Kubrick's film. King's ownership has been further asserted through the publication of the sequel book *Doctor Sleep* in 2013, thirty-six years after *The Shining* was published.

As Greg Jenkins points out, King's attitude to Kubrick's film changed from the time of its initial release (evident in *Danse Macabre* of 1981) to a *Playboy* interview in 1983 (2015: 72–4). In the latter, King points to Kubrick's 'coldness' and lack of empathy with characters and audience, his inability to understand the supernatural, and how Jack Nicholson's performance was inappropriate, due to his being already manic and not descending from normality into madness as the book chronicles (see Greene 2014). In the late 1990s, as part of the deal that saw the rights to filming the novel revert to King, Kubrick insisted that the author stop disparaging his film (see Magistrale 2015: 153).

King's television miniseries looked to 'right the wrongs' as he saw them of Kubrick's adaptation, yet sections of it seem to have to work almost too hard, to the point where they simply make the viewer think of what happens in Kubrick's version. The Torrance family appear more consolidated as a unit than in Kubrick's film, with Jack played by the more everyday and affable Steven Weber, Courtland Mead the more precocious and somewhat older Danny (he was ten years old during production) and Rebecca De Mornay as a much stronger and more resourceful Wendy. Hallorann is played by Melvin Van Peebles, a cult actor known for starring in as well as directing the startling Blaxploitation film *Sweet Sweetback's Baadasssss Song* (1971). It had something of a coup securing prominent actor Elliott Gould as Ullman, whose role was expanded more in line with the book. Aspects of the book excised by Kubrick and Johnson are reasserted: Jack's problem with the wasp's nest returns and he spends much time poring over the hotel's history through its scrapbook and cuttings; his degeneration involves him becoming more like his overbearing and violent father and he wields a croquet mallet rather than an axe; the hotel is destroyed by its 'creeping' boiler exploding and Dick Hallorann survives;

the sinister topiary moves thanks to CGI technology, and the maze has gone. An interesting innovation was to have Tony appear on screen as an older boy, who turns out to be an older version of Danny. The miniseries concludes with a 'happy ending' where Danny/Tony graduates from university in front of Wendy and Dick Hallorann, as well as the seemingly proud ghost of his father.

To take the story back very directly to its origins, King had the miniseries set at the hotel where he had stayed and became inspired to write *The Shining*. The Stanley Hotel at Estes Park, Colorado, was used for exteriors and some interior shots. To a degree, the smaller, more intimate spaces displace the large empty spaces of the more imposing Overlook in Kubrick's film. Like a number of Stephen King's television miniseries adaptations, it was directed by Mick Garris, and its four hours and 33 minutes running time gave it ample space to develop certain aspects in more detail than a shorter feature film. King reasserted his authorship not only though taking the story back to the original book but also through appearing himself in a cameo as a musical bandleader in one of the flashback sequences.

But there remains a palpable tension between Kubrick's film and King's novel and miniseries. *The Shining* certainly continues to have a notable cultural influence. However, its persistence is more down to Kubrick's *images* than King's story.[13] At least partially, this is of course due to the way that images are more easily pervasively distributed and remembered. Posters of images from the film are easily bought, and events are easily parodied, whereas King's original story is pushed somewhat into the background. For instance, not only have Universal added *The Shining*'s maze to their Halloween Horror Nights events (see Diaz 2017), but the Stanley Hotel, which inspired Stephen King to write the original book has also opened a maze in its garden inspired by *The Shining*. Seemingly missing the double-irony that the maze does not appear in the novel an online comment from a *Telegraph* reader expressed surprise that Stephen King was not invited to its opening (Anon. 2015).

The appearance of King's 'remake' was almost immediately followed by Kubrick's death in 1999, just before the opening of his final film, *Eyes Wide Shut*. In 2007, the Kubrick Archive was established as a special collection at the University of the Arts in London, which has been a stimulant to further scholarship about him and his films. It consists primarily of paperwork, and illustrates the degree of background research Kubrick went into for his films. Indeed, the pre-production stage for Kubrick's films usually took a number of years. The archive includes materials pertaining directly to *The Shining* and his other films, such as scripts, plans and diagrams, while also including much of the background work and detail about the films Kubrick never got around to making, about which he was rigorous in classifying and keeping documentation. Jon Ronson's television documentary *Stanley Kubrick's Boxes* (2008) shows the astounding degree of research and accumulation of material that was central to the way the director worked. He was loath to throw anything away. The archive contains a wealth of material pertaining to *The Shining*, including various stages of the script, memos related to shooting, editing and developing of film (including 'camera reports and lab sheets'), as well as correspondence with companies that were doing foreign dubs for the film. There are handwritten notes about Stephen King's novel as well as a fully-typed out manuscript of King's novel which Kubrick had annotated. There are some more surprising materials, such as a student thesis in French from 1991 about the narrative function of space in *The Shining*, and also a translation of *The Shining*'s script into Catalan. Along with just about everything else, Kubrick also kept reviews and any later material relating to his films, in fact almost any related material was archived. Kubrick's reputation has been bolstered internationally by the Archive sending a touring exhibition around the world.

THE SHINING'S CURRENT CULTURAL PROFILE

As I was writing this book, a newspaper story caught my eye. Apparently, according to his brother, record producer and internationally-known TV talent show panellist Simon Cowell was the axe wrangler on *The Shining* (see Wardrop 2017). This story has been around for a while and you would be prudent to be sceptical. Apocryphal or not, the appearance of a story such as this in the mainstream media is testament to just how well known Jack and his axe are, nearly four decades on. Indeed, attempting to enumerate instances of the film's referencing or parody is a daunting task.

An early instance was in *MAD* magazine (issue no. 228 from April 1981). This featured 'The Shiner', a direct comic strip parody of *The Shining*. Interestingly, Kubrick kept a copy of this issue, and it is still held at the Kubrick Archive in London. By the 1990s, the film was being parodied by TV cartoon *The Simpsons* in a sixth season (1994), episode 'Treehouse of Horror V'. This section is called 'The Shinning' and replaces the Torrances with the Simpsons, It includes a succession of scenes that are instantly recognisable from the film, with an opening that mimics the aerial shot of the car on the road and music that sounds like the *Dies Irae* melody in Wendy Carlos's music.

The Shining has had an impact in music, although in most cases slightly (or more) outside the mainstream. Allegedly, Kate Bush's song 'Get Out of My House' (on the album *The Dreaming*, 1982) was inspired very loosely and indirectly by aspects of King's book rather than Kubrick's film, but there is far more evidence of the film's influence on music. Influential

British underground metal band Head of David were an early instance with their 1986 song 'Jack Nicholson' (lyrics include 'Did you ever finish the book, Jack?') inspired directly by the film. Other rock bands have also been inspired by Kubrick's film. Masked metal band Slipknot's music video for 'Spit It Out' (2000) mixes images of the group re-enacting moments from *The Shining* interspersed with footage of them performing on stage. It starts with the band's name written backwards on the door like 'Redrum' in the film. In 2006, Thirty Seconds to Mars' music video for 'The Kill (Bury Me)' used imagery from *The Shining*, including some similar locations and restaging of some of the film's famous scenes. Most recently, Ice Nine Kills' 'Enjoy Your Slay' (2017), a song based directly on *The Shining*, the result of the band asking fans whether they should write a song based on that film or *Psycho*. The music video showcases elements from *The Shining* as well as helpfully subtitling the song's lyrics (including making them appear on the film's typewriter).

Digital recording technology has made the appropriation of samples of sound and music from elsewhere an easy task. *The Shining* has been particularly fruitful for those wanting to make a reference to, and use some impressive sounds from, a well-known film. For instance, Jack shouting 'Here's Johnny!' was used by electronic dance music act Hocus Pocus, deriving its title from Jack's outburst. The same burst of dialogue was used by Onyx and Dope D.O.D. in their song 'Stacking' (2017). British band Space used a sample of Lloyd the bartender speaking on their 'Mister Psycho' (1996), while Jack threatening Wendy was used by Nasenbluten in their song 'Cut Her to Bits' in 1995. Avant garde electronica artist The Caretaker has made albums inspired directly by *The Shining*, most notably *Selected Memories from the Haunted Ballroom* (1999) and *Stairway to the Stars* (2001). These take song recordings from the 1920s and 1930s and treat them using electronic echo, reverb and distortion to give a strange, ghostly effect. The Caretaker is one of the incarnations of James Leyland Kirby, who also has released music under the name V/VM, where he also treated old recordings electronically. The two albums mentioned sound like the sort of thing that might have been used for a soundtrack to *The Shining*, and also are slightly reminiscent of the reverberant ghostly organ music in *Carnival of Souls* (1962).

Individual images and scenes from *The Shining* have regularly been parodied and referenced in film and television, most notably Jack axing his way through the door and shouting 'Here's Johnny!', his repetitive typed manuscript, Danny writing 'Redrum' on the door, Danny on his tricycle going down corridors, the Grady girls in the corridor, or elevators bursting with blood. There are too many instances of references and homage to list here, but a few instances include: the Madonna vehicle *Who's That Girl?* (1987) sees a sequence where 'Redrum' is sprayed on a Rolls-Royce; 2016's *The Angry Birds Movie*, an animated film based loosely on a mobile phone game, briefly includes two pigs dressed as the Grady girls, who say 'redrum'; Pixar's *Toy Story 3* (2010) has some references to *The Shining*, director Lee Unkrich's favourite film, including a plethora of 237s peppered throughout in number plates, usernames and elsewhere. Unkrich runs a website dedicated to *The Shining* (theoverlookhotel.com) and helped produce Rodney Ascher's *Room 237*.

A more sustained impact was evident in Robert Ryang's edit of *The Shining* into a trailer for a mock romantic comedy called *Shining* (sometimes called *The Shining Recut*), which won top prize at the AICE's 'Trailer Park' event in 2005. Ryang took images from the film to suggest a building relationship between Jack and Danny, pivoting on a single piece of added dialogue from outside *The Shining*, 'I'm your new foster father' (Nicholson speaking in the film *About Schmidt* [2002]), and stereotypical goofball comic music succeeded by Peter Gabriel's 'Solsbury Hill' as an emotional conclusion. The prize it won was established by an international association which represents the interests of independent post-production companies, challenging editors to convert footage of existing films into trailers for a film of a totally different genre. This and many more such films in its wake are now prominent and extremely popular on the Internet.[14]

In 2016, Oregon-based hip hop artist Aesop Rock accompanied his album *The Impossible Kid* with a low-tech remake of *The Shining* as an extended music video, following most of the film precisely using basic miniature models and home-made sets. It is 48 minutes long (the length of the album) and the material in the music is in no way synched and not even related to the film action.[15] In the UK, 4Creative's startling trailer for TV channel More4's Kubrick Season in the summer of 2008 was meticulous in its copying of *The Shining*, a continuous Steadicam shot of what appears to be 'backstage' of *The Shining*'s production, with actors and technicians in preparation, that is eventually revealed to be a point of view shot from Stanley Kubrick as he is handed a script. It is absolutely outstanding in its restaging.[16] *The Shining* has been copied for comic effect in a number of television advertisements. In the USA, there was a Bing. com commercial in 2009 that parodies the film; a 'Got Milk?' commercial very directly imitates the film, with sisters, a boy on a tricycle, a voice like Danny's rendering of Tony and some music from the film and even some from Wendy Carlos's unused score; while an advertisement for Grain Belt Beer has Jack Torrance hack open a cupboard with his axe to get himself a bottle of beer. Kubrick's film has been influential outside Britain and America. Yeqi Zhu (2017) points to Juno Mak's highly referential film *Rigor Mortis* (2013), which not only makes many allusions to its predecessors in Hong Kong horror films of the 1970s and 1980s, but also makes some pointed references to *The Shining*.

Television and video games have also made references to Kubrick's film. For instance, in its opening episode, cult British TV comedy *Spaced* (1999) has main characters Tim and Daisy look at a flat and see twin girls in a cupboard. They are girl guides and say 'forever, and ever and ever' alongside flash intercutting of a red image. In the *South Park* episode 'A Nightmare on Facetime' (Season 16, 2012) Randy Marsh buys a video rental shop and after speaking with ghosts ends up acting like Jack Torrance. The opening episode of *Hannibal* (2013) has a conversation take place in a red and white toilet modelled directly on the one in *The Shining* where Jack and Grady talk (see Mee 2017: 96). In terms of video games, *Silent Hill 2* (2001) has a poster for *The Shining* on a wall, while *Fallout 3* (2008) has blood on the walls and a tricycle in the hallway in the Tenpenny Tower third-floor apartments. Episodic action adventure game *Alan Wake* (2010) has a section where the eponymous novelist character axes down a door and mentions Jack Torrance. However, the most extensive was a fan-made 'mod' of *Duke Nukem 3D* (1996) which added a new level based precisely on *The Shining*'s Overlook hotel, with a convincing architecture that matched Kubrick's film.[17]

The Shining has also proved inspiring for fine art. Gavin Turk's 'The Shining' from 2007 is a reproduction of the maze model in the film but made out of glass, aluminium and mirror film. There was an art exhibition inspired by Kubrick's films, 'Daydreaming with Stanley Kubrick', which was curated by James Lavelle and held at Somerset House in London, from July to August 2016. One of the most interesting exhibits was the Toby Dye installation 'The Corridor', which uses the UNKLE song 'Lonely Souls'. It is based on the story that, according to those involved before his death, Kubrick had agreed to make a music video for UNKLE. Dye includes images inspired by *The Shining*, most notably corridor footage, along with images inspired by other Kubrick films (the exhibition curator Lavelle is the main force behind UNKLE). One of the most intriguing artworks based on the film is by digital artist Claire Hentschker and called 'Shining 360', a 30-minute VR experience based on the opening thirty minutes of *The Shining*. Using a process called photogrammetry, 3D elements are developed from still images, constructed as fragments along a forwards-moving visual trajectory but including empty space and allowing the viewer to change direction within the 360 degree 3-D space.[18]

Even the most cursory search on eBay brings up a wealth of products related to *The Shining*. Apart from many posters and art (some of which is quite amateurish but charming), popular products include key rings for room 237 at the Overlook Hotel, and designs based on the carpet at the Overlook, including screen wallpapers for computers. There is also a board game,[19] a Garbage Pail kid card based on Jack and *The Shining* rendered as an Anime graphic novel by Kate Williamson at the website 'Geek Tyrant'.[20] Various publishing spin-offs include Derek Taylor Kent's book *Kubrick's Game* (2016), a novel which has a character delve into a code relating to Kubrick's life and films, Killian H. Gore's *The Shining Unauthorised Quiz Book* (CreateSpace, 2017), and finally, you can buy a copy of the book Jack is writing in the film: *All Work and No Play Makes Jack a Dull Boy: The Masterpiece of a Well-Known Writer with No Readers...* (Torrance 2008), which repeats 'All work and no play...' across all of its pages.[21]

One possible negative consequence of this seemingly endless cultural quotation of *The Shining* is that perhaps it has become too familiar. Anne Billson (2016) declared: 'The director's horror masterpiece deserves its cult status, but now after its motifs have been quoted endlessly for years, its thrills have worn thin ... I became fed up with the ubiquity of the film's tropes, the endless quotation and recycling.' So, the renewal of *The Shining* was down to a cult reaction, seeing the film as a conundrum and as a complex vehicle for unsaid ideas.

INTERPRETING CONSPIRACIES

One of the most striking things about some of the interpretations of *The Shining* is that the film's events and themes are not closely related at all to the conspiracy themes; in fact, they are almost unrelated. Such interpretation refuses the manifest material of the film – seeing the object of scrutiny as being 'about something else' – risks rendering the film's most interesting thematic and narrative aspects as irrelevant. Some analyses of the film have worked precisely in this way, where momentary aspects evident in the film are cherrypicked for significance and added together, and the film itself is almost immaterial to the discourse developed by the analyst. Of course, this process can happen to a lesser or greater degree with many forms of analysis and interpretation, but for many *The Shining* has taken on the dimension of allegory, where it ceases to be a straightforward depiction and is in reality about something else completely. While on the one hand this may enhance the film's cultural status, on the other it arguably negates the standing of *The Shining* as a film to simply recategorise it as a vehicle for esoteric ideas. Some critics think that these radical interpretations demean Kubrick's film. They see it as *what it is not*, and laud it for being *something else*. Films such as *The Shining* should not be merely dismissed as a puzzle (or as a 'puzzle film') according to Jonathan Rosenbaum (2012), who takes issue with this approach: 'everyone is a film critic nowadays. ... One way of removing the threat and challenge of art is reducing it to a form of problem-solving that believes in single, Eureka-style solutions'. Is *The Shining* (i) simply full of coincidences? (ii) Kubrick setting out 'secret messages' in a God-like manner? (iii) artistically incoherent, as a mixture of intermittent coincidence and authorial control? (iv) so ambiguous that it is open to pareidolia ('pattern recognition'; 'reading too much in')?

Kubrick certainly liked symbolism, which was evident from his other films and not just *The Shining* (see Ruwe 2000; Wheat 2000). Once an analyst is aware of symbolism and esoteric references in a film (or book, or other cultural product) they will tend to be receptive to them, but perhaps more so, they will actively seek them out. Sometimes this can lead to an interpretive madness, where extrapolations are made from almost every detail and significance is found in every corner. Furthermore, sometimes strange things happen when techniques used for analysing complex works of art are applied to more prosaic objects. I am thinking here of how a number of record covers have been construed as predicting the 9/11 attack in New York in 2001. Perhaps the most discussed are Michael Jackson's *Blood on the Dance Floor: History in the Mix* (1997), Radiohead's *Kid A* (2000) and Supertramp's *Breakfast in America* (1979).[22] Similarly, there is writing on the Internet that notes how the *Back to the Future* films 'predict' 9/11, President Trump and many other unexpected world events.

Is *The Shining* now part of this process? Where culture is forced to give up meanings that seem extremely unlikely? Is this over-analysis or 'reading too much into' the film? Using techniques for analysing complex and ambiguous art can lead to bizarre answers. I. Q. Hunter notes that theories surrounding *The Shining* are in many ways like academic modes of interpretation: 'Anyone with access to the Internet can replicate and disseminate the esoteric methods of tenured interpreters, or repeat them as farce; fans do it all the time, partly out of enthusiastic wackiness' (2016: 53). In discussing *2001: A Space Odyssey*, Jason Sperb notes that perhaps rather than the film being about interpretation (rather than about *something*), in fact it may be about *nothing*: in other words, outside interpretation itself (2006: 99). Perhaps this also goes for *The Shining*. If it means nothing, it might of course be made to mean anything and everything. Perhaps familiarity with the film, allied with its rich dislocated detail, produces a blank slate upon which we can project interests and desires.

Yet *The Shining* appears so replete with strange details and implications it is perhaps impossible not to discuss the material Kubrick has used. Interpretation is enabled by the extremely rich potential of material, and in particular in its splendid diversity, and in its prospective autonomy. This opens up the conceivable process of endless interpretation. Indeed, perhaps Kubrick uses material with too much potential and material that is 'too powerful' in that it can overpower other elements and not function as simply a backdrop (perhaps precisely like Native American interior design). Perhaps these elements can begin to overcome the foreground. Like too much spice in food, the taste of the principal ingredients can become lost. I am aware that Kubrick liked to use powerful ingredients, and would suggest that, for example, he often used music that had the capability to dominate images. He clearly liked such an effect and likely was also excited by the disruptive prospect and risk this might hold as well as its power and capability.

Kubrick's art in *The Shining* was making a film that despite seeming initially straightforward is overwhelmed by implications and ambiguities. The consequent resonance has not only extended the film's life as an object of fascination but also provided a sense of art as confusion just this side of a normal genre film. Ultimately, 'intention' is immaterial. It is nigh on impossible to deduce what Kubrick really intended but everything in the film has a cultural reference point and relates to existing culture, an approach identified with postmodernism. Such a conceptualization acknowledges that to mean anything, a film (or other cultural object) by necessity has to be composed of elements recognisable from existing cultural texts, and should be thought of as a collage rather than simply as an original object. The art then becomes how these objects are related to or differentiate from previous culture, and how they are combined. This is doubtless at the heart of Kubrick's art. However, with *The Shining* in particular he appeared to be 'playing with fire' through using objects that have many, sometimes too many, connections with and references to previous culture. These resonant cultural elements cannot be fully controlled by an 'author', with the resulting process being like putting together vaguely unstable chemicals. Indeed, the metaphor of playing with chemicals is a good one: intentions are easily overtaken by unforeseen reactions.

The Shining's executive producer Jan Harlan said of the film: 'of course Stanley wanted it full of ambiguity. Nothing had to make sense because the whole story doesn't make sense – it's a film about ghosts. ... Stanley really liked that idea of making a film where everything is completely confused' (in Wigley 2015). This is confirmed by Geoffrey Cocks, whose assessment was that Kubrick aimed to 'stimulate and interact with impressions and insights generated by viewers – or "readers" – of his films. It was for this reason that Kubrick would never explain his films' (2004: 6). I would go further and state that the key to *The Shining* is that it is not a controlled unity but rather its strength comes from the combination of different powerful but ambiguous objects.

The Shining is a matrix of ambiguities which has begged painstaking approaches to interpretation, and thus furnished the film with a singular cult reputation and a unique status in cinema more generally. As Richard Schickel noted in an early review of *The Shining* in *Time*, 'This is a movie of false clues and red herrings. It is a measure of Kubrick's artistry that he states his only supernatural theme, that of reincarnation, so lightly that it could be missed entirely' (1980: 69). Similarly, Janet Maslin's review in the *New York Times*, noted that this was a subtle film that required repeat viewing and would yield more material upon closer inspections (1980: C1). Kubrick's overriding concern with building a feeling of uncanny in the audience might well have led to somewhat less concern with fragmentation and connections made between diverse material held within the confines of the film.

Discussing video game *Enter the Matrix* (2003), Henry Jenkins notes that the more we try to look deeper, the more secrets appear to be revealed: 'The sheer abundance of allusions makes it nearly impossible for any given consumer to master the franchise totally' (2006: 99). This could be a description of *The Shining*, and it could be that the film was an early instance of the over-allusive constant referencing of some more recent (often self-consciously 'cult') culture. However, there is a powerful physical imperative to interpretation. Discussing extremely complex perceptual abstractions in films, Torben Grodal notes:

> I have called ... experiences that activate perception in relative isolation from other experiences and in relative isolation from distinct emotional content intense. Intense feelings may often seem to indicate some hidden meanings, because built-in mechanisms are preset to try to find some figurative meaning and recruit some meaningful associations down the line. (2009: 250)

Grodal goes on to discuss what he calls 'saturated' experience of overwrought stimulus, well beyond perception normality; that is, available in lyrical, engaging film sequences and essentially emotional in character: 'there are no action patterns available that can transform the feelings into action-oriented emotions. Such saturated associations may be felt as possessing very deep meaning' (2009: 250). Grodal's description of film interpretation from the point of view of neurology and cognitive psychology suggests that the sense of profound experience may essentially be due to perceptual matters and the tendencies and limitations of the human brain. This might account for ecstatic religious experience as well as a sense of profundity found in complex and confounding audiovisual culture such as Kubrick's film. After all, humans have an innate 'pattern finding' drive that can often lead to pareidolia, which is the discovery of what appear to be recognisable patterns in random configurations (see Donnelly 2014: 79). This is what the Rorschach blot test relies upon, as well as the phenomenon of seeing the face of Jesus in and on various prosaic objects. We look for meaning and assume that sense is there to be made.

Once an interpretation is adopted then all is approached merely as a possible addition to that interpretation, negating all other material and context. Perhaps at times this seems like archaeology, where digging takes place at random and mixes strata leading to strange conclusions. But at others, this seems like it is giving insight and clarity to fragmentation and incoherence. I do not want to suggest that all these interpretations are delusion. Far from it. In fact, the degree of close analysis is often highly impressive indeed. I am reminded of the phenomenon of 'Ripperology', the rich and diverse culture of investigating the Jack the Ripper murders of 1888 in London, often with the aim of proving the identity of the serial killer. This also has its own culture of publication and Internet presentation and debate. It also has similarly obsessive analysis, often by 'amateurs', yet the best of it is absolutely compelling and close to scholarship, while some of it is also massively intertwining and imaginative. It also has a persistent strand that alights on conspiracies.

Which interpretations of the film do I believe? All – and none. *The Shining* concludes with an ambiguity that seems to demand that we attempt some level of interpretation.

THE FILM'S FINAL SHOT: THE 'APPENDIX'

The biggest question mark is that left by the final shot of the film. The closing sequence in any film is crucial to its understanding and *The Shining*'s *appears* to offer a solution to some of the questions the film poses. It consists of two forward tracking shots tacked together and succeeded by closer still images of a framed photograph on the wall of the hotel. This sequence has a notably different character and tone from the preceding scenes of the film. Indeed, it is utterly disconnected from the rest of the film, and appears as something of an afterthought, following the narrative conclusion with the death of Jack in the frozen maze. This feeling is cultivated through details. Earlier in the film we see this configuration of photographs on the wall twice. In each case, they are different from the final grouping of photographs, and have a red sofa in front of them. So, when does this take place in relation to the rest of *The Shining*? Indeed, this sequence could arguably have been placed at the start of the film just as easily as at the conclusion. It could also easily be left out of the film, or existed on its own – something like the celebrated point of view shooting cowboy in Edwin S. Porter's *The Great Train Robbery* (1903). The sequence could take place at the same time as the action of the film, in the past (as far back as 1921) or indeed, in

Figs. 17 & 18: Slow tracking towards the photograph dated 1921

the future. Or, it might take place in a 'no time', a vacuum of progression, in 'hotel time'.

Again, psychology is implied in the film style. *The Shining* is characterised by the use of long slow tracking shots, often moving forwards, and by the use of wide-angle lenses, and extremely slow crossfades. In this final sequence, we have one long tracking shot in to the picture followed by two crossfades that show us Jack Torrance at the centre of a group of formally-attired revellers. After holding the close up of him the frame moves downwards to the writing to tell us this was the Overlook's 4th July celebration in 1921. Here, as noted earlier, Kubrick uses what David Bordwell has called parametric narration (1985: 274–9), which can supply a mechanical and dislocated sense both emotionally and narratively. The camera movement is decided and motivated by the director's abstract desire rather than pursuing the illusion of actors and events. The effect is to 'downplay content'. We do not need the shot moving gradually into the picture to get the informational point of the sequence. Like the room 237 sequence, sound and vision are divided, with the song having an ambiguous source. Is it incidental non-diegetic music? Or is it in fact a ghostly emanation from the past that is playing in the Overlook as we are watching? The film has set up the hotel as a sort of 'dead time' eternity: Jack says he has a feeling of *déjà vu* at the Overlook, and later says he wants to stay forever. This could be confirmation of the supernatural nature of the film's narrative, either through ghostly 'incorporation' or through some sort of reincarnation. The 1921 still photograph is a strange high-angle shot of a large room with a high ceiling, and what look like high society people celebrating self-consciously for the camera. It is probably the last place that a caretaker would be, let alone at the front and in the middle as if the star of this party.

The Shining appears to finish, then, with a sensational non-sequitur, an almost arbitrary conclusion that provides something of a shock. As such, it is a little reminiscent of Brian De Palma's astonishing end to his adaption of Stephen King's *Carrie* (1976) and possibly the most oblique reference to another of King's stories that was taken away from him by an authorial film director. The final sequence functions as a last-minute ambiguous statement to make the audience realise that the film poses enigmas rather than wanting to finish with a closure. A final joke, perhaps, left by Kubrick is the way that the Al Bowlly song continues as the end titles roll and they hold long enough for us to hear the clapping at the end of the recording, as if we have been watching a stage melodrama and we are reminded that we should applaud the artifice of the fantasy we have just been watching. So, rather than providing a solution or a sense of closure for the film, the ending remains open and suggests that the film should be approached as a more abstract construction, which demands the application of the intellect as much as emotions. It requires interpretation.

ASSESSING IMMERSION CRITICISM

So-called 'Immersion Criticism' might be a particularly 'cult' approach to film analysis. In the case of *The Shining*, this appears to have produced a sense of a CULT film rather than a cult FILM, perhaps. The approach to *The Shining* as a cult film has had little impact in academic writing. While there are some scholarly analyses of the film, often inspired by Kubrick as auteur, there are far more 'para-academic' arcane analyses which apply an almost Biblical level of exegesis to the film. Some films really seem to demand more thought and speculation, and *The Shining* is one of these, with its succession of nagging ambiguities and elements appearing to point outwards from the film to seemingly unrelated places.

My own initial response to conspiratorial readings of *The Shining* was one of scepticism and incredulity. However, increasingly I think it untenable that these approaches should be ignored or marginalised by serious study of the film. Yet they should also not be treated as merely a social phenomenon, enabled by the Internet's ubiquity allowing a voice to anyone, and by people with too much leisure time on their hands. That would reduce this level of interpretation of *The Shining* to a freak show observed by all-knowing anthropologists. I am sure there is something to be written about *The Shining*'s interpretations as a social phenomenon but I find the interpretations themselves more interesting, particularly as they make me address aspects of the film to which I had not previously paid enough attention.

As I have noted, many of the theories that surround *The Shining* are definitely conspiratorial and perhaps Promethean in nature. They are premised upon Kubrick encoding secret messages in a film which does not purport to hold any. Although the very term 'conspiracy theory' has a dismissive, pejorative meaning in mainstream media and culture these days, there certainly has been much evidence over the years that substantial conspiracies exist and have thrived for years before detection (or not being detected, as the case may be).[23]

These days it is difficult *not* be paranoid, with such a weight of evidence about lies and PR 'spinning' in the media. There is no gold standard for knowledge – everything might potentially be disproven and what we have been told might not have been true.[24] However, 'conspiracy' approaches can tend to find conspiracy wherever they look and be dictated less by evidence than by an emotional desire for certain versions of events being true. Indeed, most 'conspiracy theories' come from a disempowered position, where people are kept firmly 'outside the gates' by the gatekeepers of knowledge as power. This seems to be a central logic and dynamic in current so-called 'knowledge economies'. Dismissal of such 'outsider' theories is itself open to being deemed a conspiracy to suppress these interpretations; instead of being met with an open-minded scepticism, conspiracy theories can simply meet closed-minded dismissal if they challenge 'consensus' beliefs. Conspiracy theory offers an alternative to the official or 'mainstream' story of events. So when sceptics debunk a conspiracy theory they are just reinforcing the dominant 'establishment' view – not being sceptical. Indeed, the dominant 'reality', that of international media corporations and governments, aims to put all 'conspiracy theory' together in the same basket as at best misguided and at worst simply crazy.

Understanding something as a conspiracy requires agency. Someone has to be responsible. It may be Kubrick, or it may be more nebulous groupings such as the Illuminati, or simply a culture that wants to forget the evils of the past upon which the present is built. Conspiracies need an author, and in some cases, they are the results of a secret plot by conspirators of almost superhuman power and cunning. For many of the devotees of radical analysis of *The Shining*, such a description appears to describe the film's director Stanley Kubrick perfectly. As Chuck Klosterman notes when discussing immersion criticism and film:

> Now, there's a reason all these examples come from Kubrick films: Immersion Criticism only works if you believe the director really did have some type of secret objective. You have to operate from the position that the film's creator is a genius who's using the medium in a profound, personal, noncommercial manner; it also helps if the director is reclusive and refuses to answer questions about what his work means. (2013)

The assigning of overwhelming, God-like control and agency to Stanley Kubrick in many immersion criticism analyses, seems on the way to canonising Kubrick. It is clear that he included elements that are superfluous to *The Shining* as a mainstream horror film and point to strong ideas and interests elsewhere. I remain convinced that Kubrick knew what he was doing in setting up many details that cohere separately from the film's narrative but I am not convinced that all these were placed precisely by him and that a 'truth', an achievement of 'what *The Shining* is really about' is possible. Does it matter if Stanley Kubrick did not intend everything that can be found in *The Shining*? I do not see why it does. The phenomenon of interpretation of the film is both fascinating and thought-provoking, and underlines the possibilities of understanding popular culture as an almost religious bearer of social trauma and fabulation of current modes of power and existence. Much so-called 'conspiracy theory' seems to inhabit the realm of (fertile) imagination and (political) opposition. In some cases, it is clear that the approach is close to desire, where the subject may be about things people *want* to believe. (Of course, the reciprocal is true, where those who are utterly cynical in the face of conspiracy or questioning the truth of the 'consensus' order of things, *want not to believe*.)

Many of these interpretations of *The Shining* are undoubtedly radical and, I would suggest, have something in common with so-called 'against the grain readings', where books or films might be interpreted with a distinct theoretical point of view – gay, feminist, Marxist, ecological, etc. This strategy provides a distinct cast on the subject of analysis, and emphasises elements that may not be prominent as well as focusing on the possibility of seeing films or books as being 'about' something different, and not following the 'consensus' dominant reading. Sometimes this can mean reading against the intentions of the author or director, and 'reading the text against itself'. A good example of this is Tania Modleski's outstanding book *The Women Who Knew Too Much* (1988), which reinterprets Hitchcock's films through focusing on female characters and using feminist-inspired analysis. She asserts that 'a book taking a specifically feminist approach can provide a much-needed perspective on Hitchcock's films. Indeed, there are many questions that I think begin to look very different when seen by a woman' (1988: 14). A good summary of the approach is supplied by Aspasia Kotsopoulos, in her article 'Reading Against the Grain Revisited' (2001), where she points to cultural objects being made up of a hierarchy of discourses where one is dominant and others might be 'given their voice' to remove the dominant viewpoint of the film.

The Shining appears to offer up clues, demanding some level of speculation and interpretation, and so-called immersion criticism has filled a void left by scholars, for whom detailed interpretation and being in awe of the creativity and control of auteur directors had fallen out of fashion. In the 1960s, Susan Sontag wrote an influential and controversial article 'Against Interpretation', criticising interpretive approaches where any art object is shoehorned into an existing theory (such as Marxism, psychoanalysis, etc.) (2009). This can often render cultural objects as unimportant, unless they gain value as exemplars of the theory being expounded. Much of this immersion criticism has far more in common with Walter Benjamin's notion of 'immanent criticism' where analysis takes place following clues given by the object itself, and on its own terms (see McCole 2000: 89–90). However, Sontag was also wary of interpretations which do not deal with their subject of analysis on its terms and end up making it into something else. This is a tendency for much of the conspiracy-led analysis, where *The Shining* is seen as an inert agent for fragments of something totally different. Some, like Rob Ager, really do not like the term 'conspiracy theory' being appended to their analysis. I can see why, as the term is generally considered pejorative. However, I like the term 'conspiracy' or 'conspiracist' as this is not so inaccurate and describes the fanatical crusading to find what has been hidden away. Roger Luckhurst has described the radical interpretations as 'paranoid' (2013: 11), which follows a tradition in literary criticism (see Kosofsky Sedgwick 2003). Yet this seems to suggest a psychological problem with those propounding such analysis, analysis that is 'outside the gates' of acceptability in academia. Perhaps it is still outside the gates, but no longer fully ignored, and to some degree taken on its own terms.

John Fell Ryan, who refers to himself and other interpreters of *The Shining* as 'seekers', notes: 'Scores of people have written thousands of words trying to explain *The Shining* in great detail – all of whom have different points of view, and none of whom cover "everything", none of whom have discovered the Higgs boson of the film. The more you look, the less you know' (2012). I have to agree. Interest, academic and beyond, is in Kubrick's film rather than King's book. Indeed, the fuel for the interest comes from the margins of Kubrick's film where there are rich implications and intimations of metaphor and allegory, as well as a seeming deluge of references that seem to point to things outside the film, and continue to do so.

NOTES

1   Indeed, to an extent this book also has a fragmented and non-linear approach and character. This is partly a reflection of the film itself, but also an attempt to get away from approaching it chronographically as a story from start to finish. The film itself does not seem to want us to do that.

2   *Playgirl* aimed to show naked men, the same way as *Playboy* depicted naked women. Although the target group for the magazine was women it had a significant following from gay men.

3   Although apparently the MGM-owned Borehamwood Studios, also on the western edge of London, was used for one sequence with Wendy and Danny at the Maze. www.studiotour.com/movies.php?movie_id=280 [accessed 11/6/2017].

4   The differences between the two versions are recounted in 'Shine on … and Out' in *Monthly Film Bulletin*, vol. 47, no. 562, November 1980.

5   www.boxofficemojo.com

6   However, there have been books focusing on the film in Italian: Marco Carosso, *Shining. Un film di Stanley Kubrick* (Falsopiano, 2006) and Giorgio Cremonini, *Stanley Kubrick. Shining* (Universale Film, 2011); French: Loig Le Bihan, *Shining au miroir. Surinterprétations* (Paris: Rouge Profond, 2017); and German: Oliver Schmidtke and Frank Schroeder, *Familiales Scheitern: Eine familien- und kultursoziologische Analyse von Stanley Kubricks The Shining* (Campus Verlag, 2012).

7   http://www.zerozerotwo.org/KUBRICK/KUBROLOGY/MAZEgate.html [accessed 15/4/2017].

8   In addition to the already mentioned books published by CreateSpace, Chris Wade's *Stanley Kubrick on Screen* (2017) was published by Lulu (aka Lulu.com), a publisher which enables and specializes in self-publication. Similarly, Carolin Ruwe's *Symbols in Stanley Kubrick's Movie Eyes Wide Shut* (2007) was published by the GRIN Verlag in Munich, which specializes in short runs of books, and works outside the traditional gatekeeping and networks of traditional publishers.

9   This also corresponds precisely with Tzvetan Todorov's discussion of 'the fantastic', which emphasizes the uncertainty and hesitation of dealing with a potentially supernatural situation (1975: 25).

10 Catriona McAvoy notes the many Gothic influences on *The Shining* (2015a). She has written a few notable articles about the influences on the film (2015b; 2015c).

11 David Bordwell (1979) notes that one of the key characteristics of art cinema as a mode is its 'episodic' structure.

12 Diane Johnson notes that Kubrick had a way of working that prioritised structure through modular scenes, focusing on an overall architecture (see Steensland 2011).

13 There are exceptions. In 2016, the Minnesota Opera staged a new opera called *The Shining* based upon King's novel rather than Kubrick's film. The opera was written by Pulitzer Prize-winning composer Paul Moravec and librettist Mark Campbell. Also, in February 2017, using an empty hotel in British seaside resort Bournemouth, an ensemble from the Arts University of Bournemouth under director David Glass, staged a performance of *The Shining* which was inspired based on King's story but included elements from Kubrick's film.

14 Including *The Shining* made into a Wes Anderson film and a David Lynch film. http://www.openculture.com/2015/06/stanley-kubricks-the-shining-reimagined-as-wes-anderson-and-david-lynch-movies.html [accessed 2/11/2017].

15 http://www.openculture.com/2016/04/watch-a-shot-by-shot-remake-of-kubricks-the-shining-a-48-minute-music-video-accompanying-the-new-album-by-aesop-rock.html; https://www.youtube.com/watch?v=PQF6x_FgnJ0 [accessed 15/11/2016].

16 Marten GO's video on YouTube is well worth looking at, too: https://www.youtube.com/watch?v=liea8tfXpvk [accessed 20/8/2017].

17 http://www.theshining2.com/download.htm [accessed 10/2/2010].

18 https://www.youtube.com/watch?v=AupAFbIRwgY&t=798s [accessed 2/11/2017].

19 http://www.openculture.com/2015/07/download-play-the-shining-board-game-co-created-by-stephen-king.html [accessed 22/3/2017].

20 https://geektyrant.com/news/2009/11/16/the-shining-anime-style.html [accessed 22/3/2017].

21 Indeed, there is also some writing software that allows you to produce your own version of this based on Jack's repeated sentence (see Hawkes 2015).

22 http://listverse.com/2017/06/13/top-10-bizarre-conspiracy-theories-about-album-cover-art/ [accessed 20/6/2017].

23 Indeed, there seems to be almost constant revelation of conspiracies. Recent ones to note include Edward Snowden's revelation of the US National Security Agency's international surveillance of (among other bodies) friendly governments and prominent world leaders who were allies and even friends of the American president. In the UK, after the death of 96 football fans at Hillsborough stadium in 1989 it took 27 years for a legal acceptance that they had died due to police mismanagement of the crowd and that a conspiracy among the police had for years tried to blame the fans for their own deaths. The campaigning families of the victims were regularly dismissed as 'conspiracy theorists' and the 'official version' was repeated regularly in some media outlets until recently.

24 While some might see this as the embodiment of Jean-François Lyotard's 'Postmodern Condition' (1984), where knowledge is valueless and the truth is relative, but it is also the embodiment of philosopher Karl Popper's scientific theory of falsification (2002). This approach is dominant in scientific circles, and attests that all knowledge has the status of being temporary rather than being the absolute, immutable truths that we once thought.

BIBLIOGRAPHY

Abbott, Kate (2012) 'How We Made Stanley Kubrick's *The Shining*', in *The Guardian*, Monday 29 October. https://www.theguardian.com/film/2012/oct/29/how-we-made-the-shining [accessed 12/2/2015].

Ager, Rob (2012) 'Kubrick's Gold Story', Part One. www.youtube.com/watch?v+IoWZEwedPkc [accessed 6/6/2016].

Alcott, John (1980) 'Photographing Stanley Kubrick's *The Shining*', in *American Cinematographer*, vol.62, no.8, August, 780-788.

Allen, Graham (2015) 'The Unempty Wasps' Nest: Kubrick's *The Shining*, Adaptation, Chance, Interpretation', in *Adaptation*, vol.8, no.3, December, 361-371.

alt.movies.kubrick Google group https://groups.google.com/forum/#!forum/alt.movies.kubrick

Andrews, David (2013) *Theorizing Art Cinemas: Foreign, Cult, Avant-Garde, and Beyond*. Austin, TX: University of Texas Press.

Anon. (1980a) 'Shining Review' in *Variety*, 8 May, 14.

_____ (1980b) 'Shine on ... and Out' in *Monthly Film Bulletin*, vol.47, no.562, November.

_____ (2015) 'Shining Hotel Finally Opens Hedge Maze Inspired by Kubrick's Film', in *The Telegraph*, 23 July. http://www.telegraph.co.uk/film/the-shining/real-maze-opens-overlook/ [accessed 20/8/2017].

Ascher, Rodney (2012) *Room 237*.

Barkun, Michael (2003) *A Culture of Conspiracy: Apocalyptic Visions in Contemporary America*. Los Angeles: University of California Press.

Baxter, John (1997) *Stanley Kubrick: A Biography*. New York: Carroll and Graf.

Bettelheim, Bruno (1976) *The Uses of Enchantment: The Meaning and Importance of Fairy Tales*. New York: Vantage.

Billson, Anne (2016) '*The Shining* Has Lost its Shine – Kubrick was Slumming it in a Genre He Despised', in *The Guardian*, 27 October. https://www.theguardian.com/film/2016/oct/27/stanley-kubrick-shining-stephen-king [accessed 28/10/2016].

Bingham, Dennis (2015) 'The Displaced Auteur: A Reception History of *The Shining*', in Daniel Olson (ed.) *Studies in the Horror Film: Stanley Kubrick's The Shining*. Lakewood: Centipede, 114–49.

Blakemore, William (1987) 'Kubrick's Shining Secret', in *The Washington Post*, 12 July.

Blouin, Michael J. (2008) 'The Long Dream of Hopeless Sorrow: The Failure of the Communist Myth in Kubrick's *The Shining*', in Tony Magistrale (ed.) *The Films of Stephen King: from Carrie to Secret Window*. Basingstoke: Palgrave Macmillan.

Bordwell, David (1979) 'The Art Cinema as a Mode of Film Practice', in *Film Criticism*, vol. 4, no. 1, 56–64.

____ (1985) *Narration in the Fiction Film*. Madison: University of Wisconsin Press.

____ (1991) *Making Meaning: Inference and Rhetoric in the Interpretation of Cinema*. Cambridge: Harvard University Press.

Botz-Bornstein, Theo (2008) *Films and Dreams: Tarkovsky, Bergman, Sokurov, Kubrick, and Wong Kar-Wai: Tarkovsky, Bergman, Sokurov, Kubrick, and Wong KarWai*. Lanham: Lexington Books.

Box Office Mojo: www.boxofficemojo.com

Brown, Garrett (1980) 'The Steadicam and *The Shining*', in *American Cinematographer*, August, at *Visual Memory*. http://www.visual-memory.co.uk/sk/ac/page2.htm [accessed 20/09/2016].

Brown, John (1992) 'The Impossible Object: Reflections on *The Shining*', in John Orr and Colin Nicholson (eds.) *Cinema and Fiction: New Modes of Adapting, 1950-1990*. Edinburgh: Edinburgh University Press.

Browning, Mark (2009) *Stephen King on the Big Screen*. Chicago: University of Chicago Press.

Bruchac, Joseph (2015) 'Frozen Hearts', in Daniel Olson (ed.) *Studies in the Horror Film: Stanley Kubrick's The Shining*. Lakewood: Centipede, 251–72.

Bruckner, D. J. R. (ed.) (2002) *The New York Times Guide to the Arts of the 20th Century*. New York: Taylor and Francis.

Caldwell, Larry W. and Samuel J. Umland (1986), '"Come and Play with Us": The Play Metaphor in Kubrick's *Shining*', in *Literature/ Film Quarterly*, vol.14, no.2, 106-111.

Carosso, Marco (2006) *Shining. Un film di Stanley Kubrick*. Alessandria: Edizioni Falsopiano.

Castle, Alison (ed.) (2005) *The Stanley Kubrick Archives*. Los Angeles: Taschen.

Ciment, Michel (1983) 'Kubrick on *The Shining*: An interview with Michel Ciment' at *Visual Memory*. http://www.visual-memory.co.uk/amk/doc/interview.ts.html [accessed 7/7/2004].

____ (2001) *Kubrick: The Definitive Edition* (trans. Gilbert Adair). New York: Faber and Faber.

Chion, Michel (2001) *Kubrick's Cinema Odyssey* (trans. Claudia Gorbman). London: British Film Institute.

Church, David (2011) 'Freakery, Cult Films, and the Problem of Ambivalence', *Journal of Film and Video*, vol. 63, no. 1, 3–17.

Cocks, Geoffrey (2004) *The Wolf at the Door: Stanley Kubrick, History, and the Holocaust*. New York: Peter Lang.

Cocks, Geoffrey, James Diedrick and Glenn Perusek (eds.) (2006) *Depth of Field: Stanley Kubrick, Film, and the Uses of History*. Madison: University of Wisconsin Press.

Collins, Floyd (1989) 'Implied Metaphor in the Films of Stanley Kubrick', in *New Orleans Review*, no.16, Fall, 96-100.

Cook, David (1984) 'American Horror: The Shining', *Literature/Film Quarterly*, 12, 1, 2–4.

Cremonini, Giorgio (2011) *Stanley Kubrick. Shining*. Turin: Universale Film.

Curtis, Barry (2008) *Dark Places: The Haunted House in Film*. London: Reaktion.

Diaz, Eric (2017) '*The Shining* Maze comes to Universal Halloween Horror Nights 2017', at *Nerdist*. http://nerdist.com/the-shining-maze-comes-to-universal-halloween-horror-nights-2017/ [accessed 20/9/2017].

Donnelly, K. J. (2005) *The Spectre of Sound: Music in Film and Television*. London: British Film Institute.

____ (2014) *Occult Aesthetics: Synchronization in Sound Film*. Oxford: Oxford University Press.

Drummerman (nd.) www.drummerman.net/shining

Ebert, John David (2015) *The Shining: Scene by Scene*. CreateSpace Independent Publishing Platform.

Egan, Kate (2015) 'Precious Footage of the Auteur at Work: Framing, Accessing, Using, and Cultifying Vivian Kubrick's *Making The Shining*', in *New Review of Film and Television Studies*, vol.13, no.1, 63-82.

Falsetto, Mario (ed.) (1996) *Perspectives on Stanley Kubrick*. New Jersey & London: Prentice Hall.

____ (2001) *Stanley Kubrick: A Narrative and Stylistic Analysis*. Westport: Praeger.

Fenwick, James, I.Q. Hunter and Elisa Pezzotta (2017) 'The Stanley Kubrick Archive: A Dossier of New Research', in *Historical Journal of Film, Radio and Television*, vol. 37, no. 3, 367–72.

Ferrara, Serena (2000) *Steadicam: Techniques and Aesthetics*. London: Focal Press.

Freud, Sigmund (1958) *The Uncanny: On Creativity and the Unconscious*. New York: Harper and Row.

____ (1964) *Moses and Monotheism* (*The Standard Edition of the Complete Psychological Works of Sigmund Freud*, vol. 23) (trans. James Strachey). London: Hogarth.

____ (1984 [1915]) 'Repression', in Sigmund Freud, *On Metapsychology: The Theory of Psychoanalysis*. Pelican Freud Library, vol. 11. Angela Richards (ed.) (trans. James Strachey). Harmondsworth: Penguin, 95–108.

Gelnis, Joseph (1970) *The Film Director as Superstar*. New York: Doubleday.

Gengaro, Christine Lee (2013) *Listening to Stanley Kubrick: The Music in His Films*. Lanham, MD: Scarecrow Press.

Marten GO (n.d.) 'A Detail You Probably Didn't See: *The Shining* 2'. https://www.youtube.com/watch?v=xNvXaubxzrE [accessed 2/3/2017].

Gray, Tim (2016) '*The Shining* Anniversary: Stanley Kubrick and his Mysterious Classic', in *Variety*, 23 May. http://variety.com/2016/film/awards/the-shining-anniversary-stanley-kubrick-stephen-king-1201763112/ [accessed 25/5/2016].

Grodal, Torben (2009) 'Film Aesthetics and the Embodied Brain', in Martin Skov and Oshin Vartanian (eds) *Neuroaesthetics*. Amityville, NY: Baywood, 249–60.

Greene, Andy (2014) 'Stephen King: The Rolling Stone Interview', in *Rolling Stone*, 31 October. http://www.rollingstone.com/culture/features/stephen-king-the-rolling-stone-interview-20141031?page=5 [accessed 1/11/2014].

Hala, James (1991) 'Kubrick's *The Shining*: The Specters and the Critics', in Tony Magistrale (ed.) *The Shining Reader*. San Bernardino: Borgo Press, 209–11.

Harmetz, Aljean (1978) 'Kubrick Films *The Shining* in Secrecy in English Studio', in the *New York Times*, 6 November. http://partners.nytimes.com/library/film/110678kubrick-shining.html [accessed 22/4/2017].

Hatch, Robert (1980) "'Shining' It Isn't', in *Saturday Review*, July.

Havis, Allan (2008) *Cult Films: Taboo and Transgression*. Lanham, MD: University Press of America.

Hawkes, Rebecca (2015) 'Shining-Inspired Novel-Writing Tool will Turn You into a "Psychotic Writer"', in *The Telegraph*, 15 July. http://www.telegraph.co.uk/film/the-shining/psychotic-writer-novel/ [accessed 1/8/2015].

Hawkins, Joan (2000) *Cutting-edge: Art-horror and the Horrific Avant-garde*. Minneapolis: University of Minnesota Press.

Herr, Michael (2001) *Kubrick*. London: Picador.

Hills, Matt (2002) *Fan Cultures*. London: Routledge.

____ (2005) *The Pleasures of Horror*. New York: Continuum.

____ (2013) 'Recoded Transitional Objects and Fan Re-readings of Puzzle Films', in Annette Kuhn (ed.) *Little Madnesses: Winnicott, Transitional Phenomena and Cultural Experience*. London: I.B. Tauris, 103–20.

Hills, Matt and Jamie Sexton (2015) 'Cult Cinema and the "Main-streaming" Discourse of Technological Change', in *New Review of Film and Television Studies*, vol. 13, no. 1, 1–11.

Hoile, Christopher (1984) 'The Uncanny and the Fairy Tale in Kubrick's *The Shining*', in *Literature/ Film Quarterly*, vol.12, no.1, 5-12.

Hughes, Philip (1982) 'The Alienated and Demonic in the Films of Stanley Kubrick: Cinemanalysis with a Freudian Technophobic Argument', in *Journal of Evolutionary Psychology*, vol.3 nos.1-2, April, 12-27.

Hunter, I. Q. (2016) *Cult Film as a Guide to Life: Fandom, Adaptation, and Identity*. New York: Bloomsbury.

Jameson, Fredric (1993) 'Historicism in *The Shining*', in *Signatures of the Visible*. London: Routledge, 112–34.

Jameson, Richard T. (1980) 'Kubrick's *Shining*', in *Film Comment*, vol. 16, no. 4, 28–32. https://www.filmcomment.com/article/stanley-kubrick-the-shining/ [accessed 16/6/2016].

Jancovich, Mark, Antonio Lazaro Reboll, Julian Stringer and Andy Willis (2003) 'Introduction', in Mark Jancovich, Antonio Lazaro Reboll, Julian Stringer and Andy Willis (eds.) *Defining Cult Movies: The Politics of Oppositional Taste*. Manchester: Manchester University Press, 1–13.

Jenkins, Greg (1997) *Stanley Kubrick and the Art of Adaptation: Three Novels, Three Films*. Jefferson, NC: McFarland.

____ (2015) 'Stanley Kubrick and the Art of Adaptation: *The Shining*', in Daniel Olson (ed.) *Studies in the Horror Film: Stanley Kubrick's The Shining*. Lakewood: Centipede, 69–114.

Jenkins, Henry (2006) *Convergence Culture: Where Old and New Media Collide*. New York: New York University Press.

Jonny53 (2008) 'What Do the Numbers Mean?' Frequently Asked Questions in *The Shining*. Sunday, 24 August. http://faqtheshining.blogspot.co.uk/2008/08/what-do-numbers-mean.html [accessed 4/4/2015]

Kael, Pauline (1980) '*The Shining* review', in *The New Yorker*, June 9, 130.

Kauffmann, Stanley (1980) 'The Dulling', in *New Republic*, 14 June, 26–7.

Kearns, Juli (2011) "So Much About Kubrick's *The Shining*: Updated Maps of *The Shining*", at *IdyllopusPress Presents*, 29 September. http://www.idyllopuspress.com/meanwhile/13834/updated-maps-of-the-shining/ [accessed 20/10/2016]

____ (2015) 'The Alex Colville Painting that Doesn't Appear in *The Shining* but is Written All Over It', at *Fun With Kubrick*. http://fun-with-kubrick.tumblr.com/post/106706328199/the-alex-colville-painting-that-doesnt-appear-in [accessed 3/1/2017]

King, Stephen (1977) *The Shining*. London: Doubleday.

____ (1981) *Danse Macabre*. London: Everest House.

Kinney, Judy-Lee (1984) 'Mastering the Maze', in *Quarterly Review of Film Studies*, no.9, Spring, 138-142.

Klinger, Barbara (2010) 'Becoming Cult: *The Big Lebowski*, Replay Culture and Male Fans', in *Screen*, vol. 51, no. 1, 1–20.

Klosterman, Chuck (2013) 'What's Behind Room 237? *The Shining*,

Immersion Criticism, and What Might be the Documentary of the Year', in *Grantland*, 29 March. http://grantland.com/features/documentary-year/ [accessed 7/6/2015].

Kolker, Robert (2000) *A Cinema of Loneliness: Penn, Stone, Kubrick, Scorsese, Spielberg, Altman*. Oxford: Oxford University Press.

____ (2006) 'All Roads Lead to the Abject: The Monstrous Feminine and Gender Boundaries in Stanley Kubrick's *The Shining*', in *Literature/Film Quarterly*, vol. 34, no.1, 54-63.

Konow, David (2013) '*The Shining* and the Steadicam', in *Tested*, 16 August. http://www.tested.com/art/movies/457145-shining-and-steadicam/ [accessed 3/4/2016].

Kotsopoulos, Aspasia (2001) 'Reading Against the Grain Revisited', in *Jump Cut: A Review of Contemporary Media*, no. 44. https://www.ejumpcut.org/archive/jc44.2001/aspasia/againstgrain1.html [accessed 20/7/2017].

Kuberski, Philip (2012) *Kubrick's Total Cinema: Philosophical Themes and Formal Qualities*. London: Continuum.

Kubrick, Christiane (2002) *Stanley Kubrick: A Life in Pictures*. Boston: Little, Brown.

Kubrick, Vivian (1980) *Making The Shining*.

Laing, R. D. (1967) *The Politics of Experience and the Bird of Paradise*. Harmondsworth: Penguin.

Le Bihan, Loig (2017) *Shining au miroir. Surinterprétations.* Paris: Rouge Profond.

Leibowitz, Flo and Lynn Jeffress (1981) '*The Shining*', in *Film Quarterly*, vol. 34, no. 2, 48–50.

Ljucic, Tatjana, Peter Kramer and Richard Daniels (eds.) (2015) *Stanley Kubrick: New Perspectives*. London: Black Dog.

LoBrutto, Vincent (1997) *Stanley Kubrick: A Biography*. New York: Fine.

Luckhurst, Roger (2013) *The Shining*. London: British Film Institute.

Lyotard, Jean-Francois (1984) *The Postmodern Condition: A Report on Knowledge*. Manchester: Manchester University Press.

Macklin, F. Anthony (1981/82) 'Understanding Kubrick: *The Shining*', in *Journal of Popular Film and Television*, vol. 9, no. 2, 93–5.

Magistrale, Tony (ed.) (1991) *The Shining Reader*. Mercer Island: Starmont.

____ (ed.) (2008) *The Films of Stephen King: From Carrie to Secret Window*. Basingstoke: Palgrave Macmillan.

____ (2015) 'Sutured Time: History and Kubrick's *The Shining*', in Daniel

Olson (ed.) *The Shining: Studies in the Horror Film*. Lakewood: Centipede Press.

Mainar, Luis M. Garcia (1999) *Narrative and Stylistic Patterns in the Films of Stanley Kubrick*. Rochester: Camden House.

Maslin, Janet (1980) 'Flaws Don't Dim *The Shining*', in the *New York Times*, 8 June, section C1, 1.

____ (2002 [1980]) 'Nicholson and Shelley Duvall in Kubrick's *The Shining*', in D. J. R. Bruckner (ed.) *The New York Times Guide to the Arts of the 20th Century*. New York: Taylor and Francis, 2819.

Mathijs Ernest and Xavier Mendik (eds.) (2008) *The Cult Film Reader*. Milton Keynes: Open University Press.

Mathijs, Ernest and Jamie Sexton (2011) *Cult Cinema*. Oxford: Wiley-Blackwell.

Mawer, Deborah (2008) '"Parisomania"? Jack Hylton and the French Connection', in *Journal of the Royal Musical Association*, vol. 133 no. 2, 270–317.

Mayersberg, Paul (1980/81) 'The Overlook Hotel', in *Sight and Sound*, vol. 50, 54–7.

McAvoy, Catriona (2015a) '"Terror ... and the Supernatural": Stanley Kubrick's Gothic Adaptation of *The Shining*', at *British Library Blogs*, 12 January 2015. http://blogs.bl.uk/english-and-drama/2015/01/gothic-shining.html [accessed 4/7/2015]

____ (2015b) 'Creating *The Shining*: Looking Beyond the Myths', in Tatjana Ljujic, Peter Kramer and Richard Daniels (eds.) *Stanley Kubrick: New Perspectives*. London: Black Dog, 280–307.

____ (2015c) 'The Uncanny, The Gothic and The Loner: Intertextuality in the Adaptation Process of *The Shining*', in *Adaptation*, vol. 8, issue 3, 345–60.

McCafferty, Larry (1981) 'Talking About *The Shining* with Diane Johnson', in *Chicago Review*, vol.33, no.1, Summer, 75-79.

McCole, John (2000) *Walter Benjamin and the Antinomies of Tradition*. Ithaca, NY: Cornell University Press.

McQuiston, Kate (2013) *We'll Meet Again: Musical Design in the Films of Stanley Kubrick*. New York: Oxford University Press.

Mee, Laura (2017) *The Shining*. Leighton Buzzard: Auteur.

Modleski, Tania (1988) *The Women Who Knew Too Much: Hitchcock and Feminist Theory*. London: Routledge.

Murray, Patrick T. (2015) *Shooting Stanley Kubrick*. https://www.youtube.com/watch?v=w4zYSiPx2cA [accessed 5/4/2016].

Murphy, Bernice M. (2015) 'They Ate Each Other Up?', in Daniel Olson
   (ed.) *Studies in the Horror Film: Stanley Kubrick's The Shining*.
   Lakewood: Centipede, 219–50.

Naremore, James (2006) 'Stanley Kubrick and the Aesthetics of the
   Grotesque', in *Film Quarterly*, vol.60, no.1, Fall, 4-14.

Naremore, James (2007) *On Kubrick*. London: British Film Institute.

Nelson, Thomas Allen (2000) *Kubrick: Inside a Film Artist's Maze*.
   Bloomington: Indiana University Press.

Olson, Daniel (ed.) (2015) *Studies in the Horror Film: Stanley Kubrick's
   The Shining*. Lakewood: Centipede.

theoverlookhotel.com

Palmer, R. Barton (2009) '*The Shining* and Anti-Nostalgia: Postmodern
   Views of History', in Jerold H. Abrams (ed.) *The Philosophy of
   Stanley Kubrick*. Lexington: University Press of Kentucky.

Popper, Karl (2002) *The Logic of Scientific Discoveries*. London:
   Routledge Classics.

Rasmussen, Randy (2001) *Stanley Kubrick: Seven Films Analysed*.
   Jefferson, NC.: McFarland.

Reboll, Antonio Lazaro, Julian Stringer & Andy Willis (eds.) (2003)
   Defining Cult Movies: The Cultural Politics of Oppositional Taste.
   Manchester: Manchester University Press.

Rhodes, Gary D. (ed.) (2008) *Stanley Kubrick: Essays on his Films and
   Legacy*. Jefferson: McFarland.

Rice, Julian (2008) *Kubrick's Hope: Discovering Optimism from 2001 to
   Eyes Wide Shut*. Lanham, MD: Scarecrow Press.

Rosenbaum, Jonathan (2012) '*Room 237* (and a Few Other Encounters) at the Toronto International Film Festival, 2012'. https://
   www.jonathanrosenbaum.net/2016/09/room-237-and-a-few-other-
   encounters-at-the-toronto-international-film-festival-2012/ [accessed
   20/4/2014].

Ruwe, Carolin (2007) *Symbols in Stanley Kubrick's Movie Eyes Wide
   Shut*. Munich: GRIN.

Ryan, John Fell (2012) '11 Things You Might Not Have Noticed in
   The Shining', in *The Quietus*, July 13. http://thequietus.com/
   articles/09316-the-shining-stanley-kubrick-11-things-you-might-not-
   notice-room-237 [accessed 7/4/2013].

Schickel, Richard (1980) 'Red Herrings and Refusals', in *Time* magazine, 2 June, 69.

Schmidtke, Oliver & Frank Schroeder (2012) *Familiales Scheitern: Eine* familien- und kultursoziologische Analyse von Stanley Kubrick's The Shining. Frankfurt: Campus Verlag.

Sedgwick, Eve Kosofsky (2003) Touching Feeling: Affect, Pedagogy, Performativity. Durham: Duke University Press.

Segal, David (2013) 'It's Back. But What Does It Mean? Aide to Kubrick on Shining Scoffs at Room 237 Theories', in the New York Times, 27 March. http://www.nytimes.com/2013/03/31/movies/aide-to-kubrick-on-shining-scoffs-at-room-237-theories.html?mcubz=0 [accessed 1/4/2013].

Smith, Greg (1997) '"Real Horrorshow": The Juxtaposition of Subtext, Satire, and Audience Implication in Stanley Kubrick's The Shining', in Literature-Film Quarterly, vol.25, no.4, October, 300-306.

Sontag, Susan (2009 [1966]) 'Against Interpretation', in Against Interpretation and Other Essays. London: Penguin, 3–14.

Sperb, Jason (2006) The Kubrick Façade: Faces and Voices in the Films of Stanley Kubrick. Lanham, MD: Scarecrow Press.

Stainforth, Gordon (n.d.) 'The Shining', in 'The Kubrick FAQ' at Visual Memory. http://www.visual-memory.co.uk/faq/html/shining/shining. html [accessed 12/6/2008]

Stanley Kubrick Archive. London: University of the Arts.

Steensland, Mark (2011) 'The Shining Adapted: An Interview with Diane Johnson', at The Terror Trap, May. http://terrortrap.com/interviews/dianejohnson [accessed 23/08/2017].

Stolworthy, Jacob (2016) 'Stanley Kubrick's Daughter debunks Moon Landing Conspiracy Theory', in The Independent, 6 July. http://www.independent.co.uk/arts-entertainment/films/news/stanley-kubrick-daughter-vivian-kubrick-apollo-11-moon-landing-conspiracy-theory-a7122186.html [accessed 6/7/2016].

Studiotour.com: www.studiotour.com/movies.php?movie_id=280 [accessed 11/6/2017].

Todorov, Tzvetan (1975) The Fantastic: A Structural Approach to a Literary Genre, trans. Richard Howard. Cleveland, OH: Case Western Reserve University Press.

Torrance, Jack (2008) All Work and No Play Makes Jack a Dull Boy: The Masterpiece of a Well-Known Writer with No Readers. Milan: Gengotti.

Vincent, Bev (2015) 'The Genius Fallacy', in Daniel Olson (ed.) Studies in the Horror Film: Stanley Kubrick's The Shining. Lakewood: Centipede, 293–310.

Visual Memory: www.visual-memory.org.

Wade, Chris (2017) *Stanley Kubrick on Screen*. Morrisville: Lulu.

Wang, Ya-Huei (2011) 'Archetypal Anxieties in Stanley Kubrick's *The Shining*', in *k@ta*, Vol. 13 Issue 1, June, 112-122.

Wardrop, Murray (2017) 'Simon Cowell polished Jack Nicholson's Axe for *The Shining*', in *The Telegraph*, 20 August. http://www.telegraph. co.uk/news/celebritynews/5247331/Simon-Cowell-polished-Jack-Nicholsons-axe-for-The-Shining.html [accessed 27/8/2017].

Webber, Jeff (n.d.) *The Shining Code*. https://www.youtube.com/ watch?v=1oBG-f3c5EU

Weidner, Jay (n.d.) http://www.jayweidner.com/.

_____ (2015) 'Secrets of *The Shining*, Kubrick and the Moon Hoax', in *Paranoia: The Conspiracy Magazine*, issue 63.

Weishaupt, Isaac (2014) *Kubrick's Code*. CreateSpace Independent Publishing Platform.

Westerbeck, Jnr, Colin L. (1980) 'The Waning: Stanley Kubrick's Grandiose Hotel', in *Commonweal*, vol. 107, no. 14, 430–40.

Wheat, Leonard F. (2000) *Kubrick's 2001: A Triple Allegory*. Lanham, MD: Scarecrow Press.

Whittington, Paul (2012) *The Shining Revealed: An In-Depth Guide to Understanding Stanley Kubrick's 1980 Film The Shining*. CreateSpace Independent Publishing Platform.

Wigley, Samuel (2015) 'Producing *The Shining*: Jan Harlan on Kubrick', *BFI News*. 1 June. http://www.bfi.org.uk/news/producing-shining-jan-harlan-kubrick [accessed 20/7/2017]

Wlasenko, Olexander (n.d.) *Curator by Day* blog. http://curatorbyday. wordpress.com/tag/the-shining [accessed 16/3/2017].

Zhu, Yeqi (2017) 'Intertextuality, Synchronicity and Nostalgia: Transcultural Influence of Kubrick's *The Shining* on Hong Kong Ghost Horror', in *Screening the Past*, no.42. http://www.screeningthepast. com/2017/09/intertextuality-synchronicity-and-nostalgia-trans-cultural-influences-of-kubricks-the-shining-on-hong-kong-ghost-horror/ [accessed 22/9/2017].

INDEX

CPSIA information can be obtained
at www.ICGtesting.com
Printed in the USA
LVHW04s0822120518
576832LV00001B/1/P